ENCOUNTERING JESUS—
ENCOUNTERING JUDAISM

ENCOUNTERING JESUS— ENCOUNTERING JUDAISM

A DIALOGUE

Karl Rahner and Pinchas Lapide

Translated by Davis Perkins

CROSSROAD · NEW YORK

1987

The Crossroad Publishing Company
370 Lexington Avenue, New York, N.Y. 10017

Originally published as *Heil von den Juden? Ein Gespräch*
© 1983 Matthias-Grünewald-Verlag, Mainz
English translation © 1987
by The Crossroad Publishing Company

Printed in the United States of America

Library of Congress Cataloging in Publication Data

Lapide, Pinchas, 1922–
[Heil von den Juden? English]
Encountering Jesus—encountering Judaism: a dialogue/Karl
Rahner and Pinchas Lapide.
   p. cm.
Translation of: Heil von den Juden?
Lapide's name appears first on the original German ed.
ISBN 0-8245-0838-6
1. Judaism—Relations—Christianity. 2. Christianity and other
religions—Judaism. 3. Judaism—Doctrines. 4. Theology, Doctrinal.
5. Catholic Church—Relations. 6. Catholic Church—Doctrines.
7. Theologians—Interviews. I. Rahner, Karl, 1904–   . II. Title.
                    BM535.L2813   1987
261.2′6d—dc19   87-2177(
                                                                      CIF

CONTENTS

TRANSLATOR'S PREFACE

The dialogue that transpires within these pages between these two exemplary theologians covers the major points of divergence between Judaism and Christianity. Lapide and Rahner discuss frankly the topics that have separated these great religions—with tragic consequences at times—for almost two thousand years. As is to be expected, the two participants agree, disagree, agree to disagree, and on occasion simply talk past each other during the course of the dialogue. All of which makes for a truly extraordinary theological exchange.

Thanks are due Robert Detweiler of Emory University for his painstaking review of this translation. He eliminated a host of bad renderings and outright mistakes—and gave me the confidence to allow viscous German passages, most of which originate with Rahner, to pass over into English passages of comparable viscosity. The Revised Standard Version was used for most of the scriptural quotations and, in deference to the gender-particularity of German, sex-exclusive pronouns were reluctantly but faithfully translated.

Finally, I would like to dedicate this translation to my wife, Lindsay Wood, who makes all the difference.

Davis Perkins

FOREWORD

"The depth and richness of our common heritage involve us in particular in a kindly dialogue and trusting cooperation."

In these words of Pope John Paul II on 17 November 1980 in Mainz, we have seen a challenge and attempted to contribute to greater understanding between Jews and Christians. Twice, in July and in October 1982, we sat together in the Jesuit school in Innsbruck and conducted a dialogue that was reworked and expanded for publication. In these conversations we have together gone part of the way; we hope the reader can follow a little on this way and thereby discover what we have to give one another—the Jew to the Christian and the Christian to the Jew—to the greater glory of the one God.

Pinchas Lapide   Karl Rahner

LAPIDE:
Father Rahner, I have already conducted such a thoroughgoing dialogue with your books over the years that many pages are scarcely readable now because of all the question marks and marginal notations. Debating on paper makes for a bad debate, though. At last, I can now exchange ideas with you face to face in a "lively reciprocity," which, according to Martin Buber, constitutes the essence of true two-way dialogue. I would like to speak about the contrast/harmony of Christians and Jews, and what we have to give to one another. Also, we should reflect together on the incomprehensibility of God. We should do this as seekers who are all too painfully aware of their *ignorantia Dei*, yet are unable to stop speaking about the unknowable God. Is that agreeable to you?

RAHNER:
Yes, Mr. Lapide, we will attempt it. Where will we find a point of entry?

EXCHANGE
BETWEEN EQUALS

LAPIDE:

Christians and Jews as problematical nexus would be my first suggestion. In the so-called Declaration on the Jews of the Second Vatican Council (*Nostra Aetate*, no. 4), there is a key passage that is often overlooked. It reads: "Nevertheless, according to the Apostle [Paul], the Jews still remain most dear to God because of their fathers, for He does not repent of the gifts He makes nor of the calls He issues." In my opinion, this statement goes beyond the rejection of all "displays of anti-Semitism" that is spoken of in the same Council decree. In its implications it towers over even the Catholic recognition of Judaism as *one* of the many world religions, in which it sees the faith of Israel as an enduring divine call in the Christian scheme of things. However, because this "divine gift of grace" includes not only "the call" (Rom. 11:29) and the "sonship" (Rom. 9:4) but also "the covenants, the giving of the law, the worship, and the promises" (Rom. 9:4), we are concerned in this expression of the Council with a clear recognition of the Jewish community of faith as "irrevocable" (Rom. 11:29) recipient of the so-called divinely granted "privileges of Israel." It seems to me, this recognition can finally elevate the Christian-Jewish dialogue to a free exchange between equals. And still more. The Second Vatican Council explicitly recommends such "brotherly dialogues," not out of Christian charity, but in order to advance the "mutual understanding and respect" of Christians and Jews. This time it is therefore the Church in its conciliar entirety that urges the exchange with the Jews—not in order to be nice to them, but in order to deepen their own self-understanding and their knowledge of living Judaism. What do you say to this?

RAHNER:
Naturally I wouldn't think of contradicting the Council in the least. You surely know that this decree from which you have read developed as it is now because the Arab faction protested against the original plan. So the Declaration on the Relationship of the Church to Non-Christian Religions developed from a decree about Christians and Jews. It is naturally clear that from a Christian and Catholic perspective the relationship of the Church to the Jews on one hand and to non-Christian religions on the other should not be treated in one and the same document because these relationships are essentially different. But precisely on ecclesiastical and sociopolitical grounds, following a major controversy, it could not be otherwise. In any event, though,

> The Church of Christ acknowledges that, according to the mystery of God's saving design, the beginnings of her faith and her election are already found among the

patriarchs, Moses, and the prophets. She professes that all who believe in Christ, Abraham's sons according to faith (cf. Gal. 3:7), are included in the same patriarch's call, and likewise that the salvation of the Church was mystically foreshadowed by the chosen people's exodus from the land of bondage.

The Church, therefore, cannot forget that she received the revelation of the Old Testament through the people with whom God in his inexpressible mercy deigned to establish the Ancient Covenant. Nor can she forget that she draws sustenance from the root of that good olive tree onto which have been grafted the wild olive branches of the Gentiles (cf. Rom. 11:17–24). Indeed, the Church believes that by His cross Christ, our Peace, reconciled Jew and Gentile, making them both one in Himself (cf. Eph. 2:14–16).

Also, the Church ever keeps in mind the words of the Apostle about his kinsmen, "who have the adoption as sons, and the glory and the covenant and the legislation and the worship and the promises; who have the fathers, and from whom is Christ according to the flesh" (Rom. 9:4–5), the son of the Virgin Mary.

LAPIDE:
Hereupon in the Council decree follows an even more significant passage that points hopefully to the future. Would you be so kind as to continue reading?

RAHNER:
"In company with the prophets and the same Apostle, the Church awaits that day, known to God alone, on which all peoples will address the Lord in a single voice and 'serve him with one accord'" *(Nostra Aetate,* no. 4).

LAPIDE:
With this, then, the Christian mission to the Jews is unnecessary, for if one places the day of future religious concord in God's hands, what is the point still of human proselytizing?

RAHNER:
It is not quite so simple. The relationship of the Church to Israel may be essentially different from the relationship of the Church to the Gentile people, but I cannot therefore simply interpret the Christian mission to the Jews as superfluous. This is because it must, in its essence, be different from the mission to the Gentiles and because we do not know the day of unity between Israel and the Gentile Church. We also certainly don't know the day on which Japan as a people will actually enter the Church, and so the Church still works for the conversion of the Japanese.

LAPIDE:
If "the Church awaits the day, which only God knows," in which "all of them may call on the name of the Lord," as the prophet Zephaniah predicted (Zeph. 3:9), that does not absolutely mean a Christianization of the world. In any case, human assistance seems to me to be superfluous in this religious hope.

RAHNER:
No, I don't believe that human effort in the direction of unity between Israel and the Church is thereby superfluous because we must wait for the day of unity that

God decrees. God's sovereign decree and human effort are not mutually exclusive. The Council frequently speaks about something God alone knows without further reflection or effort thereupon being forbidden.

LAPIDE:

If God's gracious gifts are "irrevocable" (Rom. 11:29), then we Jews are still the bearers of election and God's promise of salvation, which went to Abraham, Isaac, and Jacob in days of old. We remain, then, even in the Christian world view, the irrevocable recipients of those divine promises and of the call, which, as Paul says, "belong to the Israelites" (according to Rom. 9:4–5). Why, then, is a conversion of the Jews still required?

RAHNER:

A gift of grace not repented of and God's promise do not preclude the reception of further gifts of grace or a further historical development and execution of one of the old gifts of grace. Through the promise of the old covenant a more positive relationship of Israel to Jesus is not precluded, as it was previously. For example, if I say: in the future you Jews must enter with us Christians into greater worship of the one God of the entire world, you must seek to battle false idols more radically with us—idols which even today are still unrecognized by Jews and Christians and revered by others. So then I say that also for Israel further gifts of grace and further calls are given as still unfulfilled obligations—even if the gifts of grace that Israel already has obviously remain.

LAPIDE:

But shouldn't such *further* calls come from God or be revealed by him, as for example at Sinai, without being transmitted by humans?

RAHNER:

I would be more careful there. For how would such a call from God alone arrive without being mediated through humans in some way? Do you have such a direct telephone connection to God that there is a genuine alternative between an unmediated divine gift of grace and one humanly mediated? As a Christian I affirm: what Jesus says to me is God's word itself to me, and precisely this word of God itself is mediated to me through Jesus.

LAPIDE:

For you as a Christian that makes sense—all the more as you refer here to Jesus as human mediator of a divine communication.

RAHNER:

Still, I cannot accept the radical alternative of which you just spoke. Naturally you could legitimately claim with perfectly normal Catholic theology that all the Church's missionary talk regarding the Jews will certainly have no success except at the moment when the Holy Spirit speaks secretly to the Jews in a way not yet evident and thus occurs a coincidence of external preaching and the inner word of grace. Even your prophets preached to the people of Israel and were not heard. How is this miscarriage of legitimate preaching to be explained? According to our theology of sin, two possibilities can be imagined: the possibility that the hearers sinfully closed their ears to this preaching, and the possibility that the hearers innocently could not understand the message. Even the Church's preachers to the Gentiles today must reckon with both possibilities and cannot in practice know precisely which of the two possibilities is actually the case with the hearers of the preaching.

LAPIDE:
There's no getting away from both possibilities with the Gentiles.

RAHNER:
Likewise something similar is presupposed, I believe, when the Church bears witness before Israel in legitimate preaching to him who is also the redeemer of Israel and as such a Jew according to the flesh. Naturally, in salvation history Israel has a singular position and duty that is also to be acknowledged by Christians. But that does not thereby signify that Israel's gift of grace, seen objectively, could reach its fulfillment apart from Jesus of Nazareth. For me, but also for Paul, you and your wife are redeemed in the same way as I am through Jesus Christ. Whether a Jew today accepts that or not, whether he does not accept it guiltily or innocently (which obviously is possible and would usually be the case), that is naturally another question. For me as a Catholic Christian it is self-evident and valid also for the Jews according to Paul: all have sinned and need the forgiving grace of God, which is promised to us irreversibly and with historical clarity through the Jew

Jesus of Nazareth in his cross and his resurrection. However not only for us Gentiles but also for you Jews.

LAPIDE:

That we all together and as a rule are sinners, who need the forgiving, gracious love of God, is beyond every doubt. In weakness, error, and mistakes, our ecumenicity is just as seamless as is our common dependence on God's patience and compassion. If, however, Jesus died "for us all" (Rom. 8:32) "to reconcile to himself all things, whether on earth or in heaven . . . by the blood of his cross" (Col. 1:20), how do you reduce the self-sacrifice of this Jew to the monopoly of the Church? If Paul was right, then the redemptive effect of his martyrdom belongs not only to Christians, but to the whole world!

RAHNER:

If that is the case, though, then all—including the Jews —are called and fundamentally obligated to confess explicitly this redemption through the cross of Jesus and the community of those who do that, called the Church of Jesus Christ, which should in principle envelop Jews and Gentiles.

FAITH AND ACTION

LAPIDE:

Does that mean that faith in the salvific power of the cross is indispensable for redemption or does Jesus' atoning death contain a universal efficacy even without the faith of the individual person?

RAHNER:

One must make a distinction there according to the Second Vatican Council. Obviously the person who in conscience does not say a definite no to God and God's grace is redeemed, justified, and saved in any event— and through the universal redemption of Jesus on the cross. However if, and insofar as, one recognizes this salvific situation in Jesus Christ, then one must confess this according to Christian teaching and in the religiously public way of the Church. One must allow oneself to be baptized. If one does not recognize the universal redemption through Jesus Christ and cannot extract the consequences given therewith, then this person naturally comes into the eternal life of God just like a Christian, quite as if someone in good conscience should feel obliged to take my life.

LAPIDE:

I can scarcely imagine that the grace of God, who "makes his sun rise on the evil and on the good" (Mt. 5:45), depends upon whether the individual Jew believes in him or not. It often strikes me that God also has a heart for atheists who seek him unconsciously. God's work appears to me so universal. As the psalmist says: "The Lord is good to all and his compassion is over all that he has made" (Ps. 145:9).

RAHNER:

Even there I would say once again: I make a distinction. As a quite normal Catholic-trained theologian, I can still conceive of the possibility of a final existential yes to God being given even when one believes oneself to be an atheist—and should be one—in one's everyday, verbalized consciousness. I don't think it is thereby necessary to exclude such a person from the universal and efficacious salvific will of God or to believe that many will be saved irrespective of their freedom. God would therefore save without this saving occurring through a voluntary turning to God. The power of God's grace includes even our freedom. Is that understandable? It must surely be understandable for a Jew of the Old Testament. The prophets certainly call for the free decision of the person in a radical way. A radical, universal salvific will of God (I can imagine intensely how this must befit the infinite God), which envelops even our freedom, must nevertheless not be efficacious apart from human freedom. For me no alternative exists between the universal, efficacious salvific will of God and the human freedom that God alone must bestow in order for him to be found.

LAPIDE:
You are familiar with Jesus' parable of the two sons (Mt. 21: 28–31), which is rabbinically well established. At the request of the father to work in the vineyard, the first son said "Yes, Lord"—but he did not go. Then the father turned to the second son with the same request, which he brusquely rejected. Later, however, he thought better of it and went to work.[1]

In our context today that probably means that while many a person is not ready to repeat a confession of faith still the salvific purpose of God is advanced through the work of that person's hands, whereas another says yes to the father and calls him "Lord, Lord," but does nothing in order to sacralize this world of God's. Which of the two stands nearer to our father in heaven?

RAHNER:
The first one.

LAPIDE:
Then we should grant no priority to articulated faith, but rather to actively doing "the will of my Father in heaven" (Mt. 12:50). Perhaps Goethe was right when he had the angels in *Faust* sing: "For he whose strivings never cease is ours for our redeeming."

1. Lapide actually reverses the order of the sons as given in the parable.—TRANS.

RAHNER:

You always construe alternatives that are not real. There are very different realities in the world, all of which exist and yet are not the same. Therefore a person must basically assume a definite attitude, naturally of various sorts, toward these different realities. Therefore I can construe my final redeeming relationship to God concretely through a different attitude to different realities, whereby many such different attitudes taken together can be of redemptive significance. You can give a handout to your cousin so that he does not starve; you could also perhaps allow yourself to be shot to the moon in order to study the earth, and so forth. In all of this there are naturally things in which you can essentially realize your relationship to God and which could mediate it, but they are overlooked or for other reasons you innocently don't do them. I am pretending now: I have a cousin; he is starving; I should attend to him; I don't know it, though, or I fail to do it, although I do know. In other words, there are potential imperatives, missions from God, and so forth, that one must fulfill which are different from one another. The neglect of one of these is not charged against a person by God because one does not recognize them or does not recognize them as divine imperatives.

LAPIDE:

Allow me to sharpen the question. The most frequently used verb in the preaching of Jesus of Nazareth is the verb *do*. The most frequently used phrase is the *kingdom of heaven*. That must be more than a simple accident. I can only conclude from this that the arrival of or the preparation for the kingdom of heaven in Jesus' view required human participation. Consider a humanist, who thoroughly and completely thinks only in a human-earthly way, does not believe in God, but saves thousands of his fellow human beings from starvation, from sickness, or from poverty. Across from him stands a religious Christian who prays properly, goes to mass weekly, and could give a damn about his neighbor. Which of the two surely stands closer to our father in heaven?

RAHNER:
The first one, obviously.

LAPIDE:
Then the deed that pleases God is still of greater importance.

RAHNER:
Naturally, that is self-understood. But one cannot conclude from this that the atheist who realizes that he may not be a genuine atheist must worship God in the synagogue and make himself innocent before God if he neglects this express confession of God.

LAPIDE:
That may be. Nevertheless I incline toward the opinion of the rabbi from Nazareth, who impressed upon us: "You will know them by their fruits!" (Mt. 7:16)—whereby the warning resonates for the Jews: *not* by their talk!

Faith as blind faith is not so much a onetime experience in Judaism as a lifelong antecedent, accomplishment, and effect. It does not concern itself with merit, rather with service in the kingdom of God. Not with achievements, but with love. However, love of God without actions pleasing to God is for Jews hypocrisy or empty drivel. James, the brother of Jesus, said it more bluntly: "Faith apart from works is dead" (Jas. 2:26).

God is not so much the commander of worship as the creator and governor, whom the person can truly serve through the fulfillment of the Torah, which is above all a doctrine of actions of faith. Hence the Jew says of Christianity: I certainly hear the news, but . . . allow us to wait for the ripening of the Christian fruit before we pass judgment. As far as this fruit is concerned, Jews for the last eighteen hundred years have had little reason or occasion to recognize a *communio sanctorum* in the Church. At least we must observe that it is not yet that. Christians on the other hand are mostly of the opinion that we Jews are no longer what we claim to be: the chosen people of God. Between the "not-yet" of the Church from the Jewish perspective and the "no-longer" of the Synagogue ("the *formerly* chosen people") from the Christian perspective yawns a chasm that should have been bridged.

RAHNER:
Good. You feel yourself still to be the chosen people. And we Christians can concede tearfully and despairingly that with which you reproach us. But permit me still to raise the question: How are we clearly to recognize the chosen fruit of the chosen people that you believe yourself to be?

ELECTION AND PASSION

LAPIDE:
In Judaism election is not a gift, but rather a task; no contract with God, but rather his holy mission; no honor, but rather a heavy burden which it is necessary to bear and to realize.[2] Whoever has doubts about its continuing validity should reflect upon the passion of Israel, a two-thousand-year road of suffering, and should remember keenly the servant of God who is docile "like a lamb that is led to the slaughter" (Is. 53:7).

RAHNER:
Good. However I can now say: in exactly the same way you must acknowledge the passion of Jesus (no matter who caused it) as the great unprecedented crystallization and apex of the passion of Israel and from this accept Jesus also as your redeemer.

LAPIDE:
The present pope, who for many years was also the bishop of Auschwitz, said in that death factory: "This is

2. Lapide is here engaging in a series of clever wordplays which is unfortunately lost in translation: *Gabe/Aufgabe, Vertrag/Auftrag, Würde/Bürde.*—TRANS.

the Golgotha of our age." For those of acute hearing, he thereby drew a bow of destiny that unites the Jerusalem of the year 30 with the crematoriums of the year 1945. There are pious Jews who in openly courageous dialogue with Christians would be prepared perhaps to attribute saving power to this bow—according to that old rabbinical doctrine that recognizes suffering as the loving discipline of God (Berakot 5a), as expiation of guilt (Berakot 5a), or regards it as vicarious suffering atonement for a sinful world (Berakot 62b; Moed Katon 28a).

RAHNER:

One would have to point the bow, as it were, from Auschwitz back to Golgotha, from where one can finally find an ultimate meaning in the terribleness of Auschwitz.

LAPIDE:

That Jesus suffered God's will and voluntarily gave up his life for others, I can accept as historically trustworthy. I have a hard time with the uniqueness of his martyrdom since countless of his companions in the faith—before him, on both sides of him, and also after him—had to empty the bitter cup of sorrow down to the dregs. I have no yardstick with which to compare whose suffering was greater, deeper, or more pleasing to God. For me they are all heroes of the faith in an all-too-long *passio Hebraica* that begins with the Maccabeans and extends beyond Golgotha to the carnage of the Crusaders and the bloodbaths of the self-proclaimed "avengers of the murderers of God" until after Auschwitz.

RAHNER:

I can partially understand all that, but you must still grant me that it is hard for a modern person to realize that this entire history of suffering generally has something positive to do with God. I know full well that there were Jews in Auschwitz who died with their rabbis believing and praying. Yet they also say that the majority of Jews went to the gas chambers in godless despair. Whether these, and how these, could have still found God is another question altogether. But whether one could experience, in historically tangible terms, an ultimate, positive sense in this passion is still an open question. As a Christian I would say that I can discern definitive and indissoluble evidence for the meaningfulness of the entire history of human suffering, and so also of Israel's, only in Jesus the crucified and resurrected.

LAPIDE:

Jewish history, four thousand years long and five continents wide, consists largely of an endless series of persecutions, exiles, and decimations. What resulted from this is a continuous learning process from the various defeats and a mastering of hope—coming directly out of the failures. Prophets and rabbis may certainly be reckoned as world champions in the theological interpretation of pain and suffering. That begins with the four hundred years of Egyptian subjugation and the planned genocide of the Pharaoh who wanted all Hebrew boys drowned in the Nile. It continues with the forty years of wandering in the desert, with hunger and the bloody battle to occupy the land, the destruction of both temples, the seven decades of Babylonian captivity, worldwide pogroms, Diaspora, and extends to the "Final Solution" of Hitler. This Jewish faculty for taking the sting out of death through unswerving faith and to salvage over and over again new rays of hopeful strength from out of the abyss of destruction—herein one can find the key to the mystery of the Jewish art of survival. In this sense perhaps the most Jewish element in the belief structure of Christianity is the Pauline interpretation of redemption on Golgotha.

RAHNER:
I would then like to ask: Has the average Jew of today the courage to believe in some final meaning for those who were killed?

LAPIDE:
Perhaps not all, but certainly many. As an example, take the prime minister of Israel Menachem Begin, who doesn't have much to do with theology. In response to the question of a German journalist (on 30 November 1978), whether he could still believe in God after Auschwitz, his answer ran as follows: "Yes, I do. Because Auschwitz is our sacrifice for the justice of God in this world. I believe in God's leading in politics. If Hitler had not murdered the Jews, he would, under the circumstances, have won the war. If there had not been divine providence, then Hitler would have built the first atomic bomb . . . then our world would have become a single, great penitentiary. The age of darkness had dawned. . . . We Jews brought the greatest sacri-

fice into this battle for the survival of humanity. . . . Perhaps we had to make the sacrifice in order for Hitler to lose.

RAHNER:
Yes, that is certainly wonderful. But I would still like to ask Begin: What about the Jews who were gassed in Auschwitz? There I must as a Christian say: I believe in and hope for the eternal life of God for all these people. Such a hopeful belief is simply my Christian duty. Or better, I am empowered to this wonderful hope through the grace of God in Jesus Christ.

BELIEF IN
ETERNAL LIFE

LAPIDE:

I believe with total certainty in eternal life. It belongs to my Jewish existence. The resurrection of the dead is certainly no Christian discovery; rather it is verifiably over 160 years older than Jesus of Nazareth. The small band of Maccabeans was so firmly convinced of a future life after bodily death that in defiance of death they fought so courageously they succeeded in defeating an enemy of superior military strength and winning back Israel's independence. Their belief in a Beyond was therefore in no way "an opium of the people," as the Marxists maintain, but just the opposite: a highly effective incentive for the improvement of this life. This happened about 167 B.C.E. Since this time all practicing Jews (with the solitary exception of the Sadducees, who disappeared from history in year 70 with the Second Temple) believe in the future resurrection of the dead.

RAHNER:

Does that belong to official Jewish teaching also?

LAPIDE:

Certainly. It belongs to the daily liturgy of the synagogue and is both recited as a rule of faith and sung in verse form. In the words of Maimonides, which found admittance into our prayer book: "I believe with full conviction that a resurrection of the dead will take place at the time that is pleasing to the creator." Without this Jewish religious truth as a precondition, I cannot possibly imagine the Easter experience of Jesus' disciples.

RAHNER:

Good. Let us suppose with Rudolf Pesch, for example, that in Jesus' time there already was a theory or a theology of a possible resurrection of the righteous and that this theology was helpful to the disciples of Jesus in correctly interpreting the final fate of Jesus.

LAPIDE:

There is a rabbinical reading of the near-sacrifice of Isaac that is most likely older than the epic poem of the Maccabeans. It states that Abraham was prepared to sacrifice his only son—in spite of the divine promise that was tied to Isaac's still-unborn descendants—because he had the certainty that God is able to enliven again even the dead Isaac from the ashes of his burnt offering. This confidence, that God also "keeps the faith with those who fall asleep in the dust" (as it says in an ancient prayer), and the pious interpretation of the passion—both came into the theology of the early Jewish-Christian community from the rabbinical reservoir of faith.

RAHNER:
I don't contest that at all.

LAPIDE:
You certainly should not. For one and a half millennia, Jews and Christians have placed the emphasis on their divisions. It is high time to shift it to the countless fundamental commonalities.

RAHNER:
May I say something else in between? I don't know whether Jewish theology today in legitimate self-defense sufficiently supports us orthodox Christians in our dialogue with contemporary atheism, with self-proclaimed enlightened liberalism, and so on.

TWO ISLANDS OF FAITH
IN THE SEA OF ATHEISM?

LAPIDE:

For years I have been unable to rid myself of the tormenting suspicion that Judaism and Christianity—whereby I mean neither all the circumsised nor all the baptized, but rather the faithful folk of the Bible—run the danger today of shrinking to two islands of faith in the midst of a stormy sea of atheism and materialism. Our days are reminiscent of the distressing time of Samuel, of which it was said: "The word of the Lord was rare in those days; there was no frequent vision. . . . The lamp of God had not yet gone out" (1 Sam. 3: 1, 3).

If under these circumstances we do not achieve a candid dialogue, conducted with love and empathy, about everything that unites and divides us, then the faith in our common Father in heaven is in a sorry state. Such a creative dialogue should not conceal or blur the genuine religious differences, but should rather summon up the courage to struggle to create a grand coalition of all believers, in order to provide as an example to this revelation-blinded world, alienated from God, a bit of redemptive conviction. Therefore I have come here—in order to sit together with you, not in order to argue with you.

RAHNER:
I am absolutely of the same opinion.

LAPIDE:
I would still add one thing: In the course of the drifting apart of Jews and Christians, we have made our legitimate differences *awful*—in the disdain of those of other faiths, in the arrogance of narrowmindedly monopolizing salvation, and in the self-justification that can establish its truth only by calling the other a liar. Should we not finally make our differences *fruitful*[3]—as a path to deepened self-understanding, as an invitation to see the world with the eyes of others for once, and perhaps even as a hint that God loves diversity and is sufficiently great enough to be reached not through a formula, not even through several ways, but rather through innumerable ways?[4]

RAHNER:
Yes, certainly. I am in total agreement. Only one may not understand what you said in the sense of a cheap indifference. That would, in my opinion, be neither good Judaism nor good Christianity. There are certain distinctions in the realities and also in the convictions

3. There is a German wordplay here in the use of *furchtbar* ("awful") and *fruchtbar* ("fruitful").—TRANS.

4. Lapide is engaging here in another wordplay with the German words *Einzahl, Anzahl,* and *Unzahl.*—TRANS.

according to which either can concede to the other that his opinion is precisely as good as one's own. So a black person and a white person can say of each other that black and white are just as beautiful and good and each should remain his own skin color. But regarding Jesus of Nazareth, there are conflicting positions that "objectively" cannot be mutually granted the same warrant. Over this we will dispute even further today.

LAPIDE:

Perhaps he would even want us to dispute about it further in a brotherly way. He did it often enough himself. So I would like to take you up on your public offer (in the magazine *Der Spiegel*, 21 February 1972) to subject every dogma to reason. Thus I assert that all your various Christologies are henceforth open to debate, resisting all attempts at a coerced uniformity and leaving room for a mystery that exceeds all human wisdom. You yourself are the man who explained in the Second Vatican Council that all religious truths must be constantly formulated afresh in order to meet the demands of the changing linguistic instinct and spirit of the age. I believe accordingly neither in word-splitting nor in what Martin Luther called stultified "literalism."

RAHNER:

And also, one hopes, no relativist—who makes it too easy.

LAPIDE:

By no means. For no one would be served thereby. Thus I believe that even the main divisions between

Jews and Christians are capable of being redesigned, as soon as one reflectively and empathetically scrutinizes them. If I contemplate the Incarnation in this way, it is basically neither idolatry nor deification of the creature and not at all an attempt to seize hold of God, as some Jews maintain, but in the final analysis only a further development or the taking it to its logical conclusion of that Hebrew doctrine of salvation that understands the loving bestowal of God in his humanity as the basic dynamic of all world history. What is meant is an "entering of God into humankind," as Father Willehad Eckert said. Or as Helmut Gollwitzer defines it: "The covenantal God is in solidarity with his people threatened by the judgment of death; so much in solidarity that he identifies completely with them." This involves neither the Jewish confession of the incorporeal nature of God nor a pure identity, but most certainly a mystery that no Christian can presume to fathom. The Jewish scholar André Neher says about Christology: "The Christianity whose theology is able to frighten only hypersensitive Jews appears to us to be a Jewish messianism taken to its final conclusion."

All this naturally does not mean that all distinctions may be leveled overnight, but certainly that questions like the Trinity, Eucharist, Incarnation, and parousia cannot be discussed either through a double monologue or in flashy debates. They must rather be discussed in a genuine dialogue in which both partners are unconditionally ready to launch an unrestricted search for the truth.

RAHNER:

I would gently add that the word *incarnation* is also misunderstood and can cause difficulties for even an obliging person, not for you a Jew, but precisely for a new, contemporary pagan. These difficulties are not grounded simply in the malevolence or stupidity of such a person. The God of Israel, who is also my God, does not transform himself into a human being. The word *incarnation*, "becoming human," is certainly a sacrosanct word for us that I cannot oppose, although the word *become* appears to imply a transformation from something to something in normal linguistic usage. And this surely causes certain difficulties for the modern person who would be a new believer.

THREE GODS
OR A TRIUNE GOD?

LAPIDE:

I could imagine that a Christian-Jewish dialogue about the true significance of the Trinity as well as about the astonishing traces of triads in Judaism could also prompt an intellectual rapprochement.

RAHNER:

Regarding the Trinity, some time ago in Mödling, near Vienna, I gave a lecture to Muslims (not as if I understood anything about their own theology, of course). In this lecture I attempted, from within Catholic theology, to dissolve the misunderstanding surrounding the Trinity, as if this Christian doctrine still implicitly implied three gods. I believe that on this question Jewish and Christian theology could be reconciled.

LAPIDE:

In this regard, the example of the *locus classicus* of the Jewish triadic concept would be helpful: the theophany of Abraham by the oaks of Mamre. In a brief text (Gen. 18), the transition from the threefoldness of the men to the singularity of God is so frequent and immediate that the conclusion appears almost unavoidable: God availed himself here of three men (or angels) or one of the three in order to reveal himself to Abraham the progenitor.

RAHNER:
Yes, and there is the famous icon of Andrey Rublyov.

LAPIDE:
It reminds me of the rabbinical question, Why does the Bible speak so often of "the God of Abraham, the God of Isaac, and the God of Jacob," instead of being satisfied with the shorter formulation "the God of Abraham, Isaac, and Jacob"? Why the apparently superfluous trebling of God's name, when there is still only a single God? The answer that unfolded in the course of a lengthy debate states: Abraham experienced him as the God who leads the way, who calls to him in the uncertainty of the promised land; Isaac, his son, experienced him as God the guardian, who delivered him on the mountain of Moriah from the sacrifice by the knife of his own father; Jacob, the grandson, on the other hand, experienced him as the combative angel who wrestled with him throughout the night until at dawn he could wrest his blessing from him and the new name Israel. So it rightly says in the Bible, "the God of Abraham, the God of Isaac, and the God of Jacob," for it concerns three various experiences of God, which are truly entirely different from one another and yet are nevertheless every bit as legitimate and authentic as the visions of God of the Synagogue, the Church, and the Mosque

—the three (none)-in-one *(Drei(un)einigkeit)* of the three branches of monotheism in our contemporary world.

RAHNER:
Notice that what works in your context is what I repeatedly try to clarify for my colleagues in Christian dogmatics, namely, that the economic Trinity is the immanent Trinity and naturally also the reverse.[5]

LAPIDE:
That pleases me.

RAHNER:
Yes. I think that one should not speak of an economic Trinity and then with a completely new, speculative effort distinguish that from an immanent Trinity, as if we could know and explain anything about the inner life of God. God does not communicate his inner life to us through mere speech in sentences, but rather through his authentic turning to us in grace and incarnation.

LAPIDE:
What must confuse many Jews is the abandoning of the letter *u* by the later dogmaticians. In the early church fathers it was still called *triunitas,* whereby the unity is placed in the foreground. Trinity, on the other hand,

5. Rahner is referring here to the traditional distinction made by Christian theologians between God's being considered apart from divine activity in the world (immanent Trinity) and God's being considered with respect to divine activity in the "economy of salvation" in the world (economic Trinity).—TRANS.

purely speaking, sounds like tri-theism or even like a heavenly triumvirate. In the Quran also, Mohammed understood it in this way and deplored it. In a 1972 interview in *Der Spiegel* about the dogma of papal infallibility, you said that in all probability Jesus "would not have understood it at all." Probably the same thing also goes for the subtlety of the Christian doctrine of the Trinity.

The heart of the matter lies in the fact that one can take the Bible seriously—or literally. Both together are incompatible. For all of our speaking is assuredly a human enterprise that is capable of giving expression only to our experiential world, but not to eternal truths which lie beyond all human comprehension. Moreover, languages are living realities that change constantly: new words come into them, obsolete ones are discarded, and the majority of one's vocabulary is subjected to continual semantic alterations. How can one expect Hebrew or Greek texts that are millennia old, originated in another part of the world, and belong to a long-dead thought-world to convey the same message today as then. Nicholas of Cusa is surely right when he says that all our talk of God is nothing other than helpless stammering, light years removed from any scientific precision.

RAHNER:
I frankly admit that because of linguistic developments that occurred since the time of the Church fathers— developments that even the Church could not control— the word *person*, when applied to the Trinity, gives rise today to almost insurmountable misunderstandings that

are not at all contained in the actual dogmatic formulation. But don't therefore allow the word *person* to be discarded from the doctrine of the Trinity in the ecclesiastical idiom.

LAPIDE:
One could perhaps go back to *prosopon*, which was originally a mask in Greek theater and later came to mean "face" or "countenance."

RAHNER:
Yes, but I would be very careful there. Otherwise I run the danger that my colleagues in Christian dogmatics reproach me with: that I deny the essence of the divine Trinity, that I advocate a modalism or a patripassianism. But one cannot speak dogmatically of three various persons in the Trinity in the modern sense of "person," that is, of a single, unique center of free action. This is because this modern thrust to the concept of person belongs in the dogmatic sense to the essence of God, which is established only once. But unfortunately very many people today understand the doctrine of the three divine persons in the sense of a modern concept of person and then they are tritheists, even if they don't want to be.

LAPIDE:
Could one perhaps speak of three aspects without falling into modalism?

RAHNER:

It was certainly not my own discovery (neither as far as the substance goes nor the term), but I have proposed to speak of three modes of subsistence in the doctrine of the Trinity—even if only that is named expressly which distinguishes itself through Father, Son, and Spirit, and naturally is constituted through the same divine essence. Thus the reproach of Walter Kasper—that one cannot pray to three modes of subsistence—seems to me to miss the mark.

LAPIDE:

Would it not be conceivable for us, like Jesus and the rabbis, to manage without a lot of abstractions and to remain in the concrete realm of narrative. Instead of defining the unknown essence of God precisely and properly through Greek structures of thought, would it not be simpler to remain for the present with the three various dimensions of the experience of God that characterize the faith of our partriarchs?

RAHNER:

For a Christian, there are three most fundamental experiences of the one God: Father, Son (Word), Holy Spirit. If I also say that these three most fundamental experiences are the attributes of God himself and that they distinguish themselves not simply through the mode in which God comes to me, then I say precisely that this one and the same God is in himself threefold. And therefore the economic Trinity and the immanent Trinity are the same for me.

LAPIDE:

The Jew relies upon the three fundamental experiences of God of his ancestors, to which in the course of history have been joined so many others of different sorts that all attempts at a systematic classification evoke scorn. The prophets warn us repeatedly about the manufacturing of images of God: "To whom then will you liken God, or what likeness compare with him?" (Is. 40:18) It often appears almost as if Wittgenstein was right when he said, that about which we do not know, we should keep silent.

RAHNER:

No, I am not in agreement with Wittgenstein. Christian theology is simply speech about the incomprehensible God, about which one *must* speak, though this speech necessarily and always stands at the border crossing point that leads into the silencing worship of God.

THE INEFFABLE REMAINS

LAPIDE:

Jews also speak about God, most beautifully in poetry and periphrases, in full consciousness of the theological inadequacy of all verbalizations about the Almighty.

RAHNER:

Of course one does not have to expressly append to every theological doctrine the note that it is correctly understood only when it is understood as a probe into the ineffable mystery of God. But every theological doctrine is only true then if it is so ordered and stated.

LAPIDE:

The Jewish compromise between the "must-speak-of-God" and the "cannot-speak-of-God" is the so-called awe of names. We abstain from every mention of the holy tetragrammaton by using other names of God in order not to profane it. We speak of God as Jesus did, periphrastically, as the Greatly to be Praised, our Father in Heaven, the Holy One, Ruler of the World, etc.

RAHNER:

At the beginning of the *Confessions* of Saint Augustine stands the beautiful statement (chap. 4 of the first book):

"And what saith any man when he speaks of Thee? Yet woe to them that keep silence, seeing that even they who say most are as the dumb."

LAPIDE:

When it comes to pouring out one's heart before God, almost every Jew is a Jeremiah who would surely remain silent, but in whose heart there is "as it were a burning fire shut up in my bones, and I am weary with holding it in, and I cannot" (Jer. 20:9). For many who find it urgent to contend or to argue with God, the word of Job applies: "I must speak, that I may find relief; I must open my lips" (Job 32:20).

RAHNER:

We must be united in this matter. With our talk about God we Christian theologians and pastors create the impression that we could tap God on the shoulder and are not talking about something that is only true when at the same time it is understood and worshiped as the incomprehensible mystery.

LAPIDE:

Of this inscrutability you once said with supreme irony: "What then does one know so precisely about the 'loving God'?" In fact, what we both know *about* God would fit without difficulty on a postcard. What we know *of* God fills the twenty-four books of the Hebrew Bible and the twenty-seven writings of your canon. Therefore I have an almost intuitive reservation about your voluminous dogmatics, which reminds me—if you will pardon me—of the servant Wagner in *Faust* who wanted everything "black and white." Perhaps we should have less dogmatics, but more *diogmatics*—from *diokein*, "chasing," "pursuing" (*diogmos:* the object of the hunt). This in the sense of Paul, who at the end of his life possessed the spiritual greatness to be able to say of the mystery of faith: "Not that I have already obtained this . . . but I press on" (Phil. 3:12).

RAHNER:
One can certainly understand what you said properly and endorse it and even attempt to translate it into theological praxis. But for me as a Western philosopher (if I am one), it is a matter of propositions, to be formulated via "more and less." If someone says there should be "less" dogmatics, then I ask myself, must there be no more dogmatics or only "less" dogmatics? And if there should still be dogmatics (even if less), then we have the same problems, which should be avoided with this advice.

LAPIDE:
If only dogmatics summoned up the courage to confess that in the final outcome it is continually speculative; if it could say with Karl Rahner that change also belongs to its essence, so that one may assail and interpret anew its formulations—much would be won for the dialogue. Conclusively and finally, it was certainly said even of Jesus that he "grew and became strong in spirit" (Lk. 1:80) and "increased in wisdom and stature" (Lk. 2:52). What should also be said probably is that he thereby learned he must change his opinions, here and there let

himself be told something, and be prepared to rethink it.

RAHNER:
I once said after the Council that, if all profound theology during and after the Council remained self-absorbed and did not pass over into the practice of the worship of God in everyday life, it would be like having a massive pile of uranium ore that produced no radium.

LAPIDE:
I am in agreement with that. For even the best theology constantly runs the danger of becoming altogether too "cerebral" as an intellectual undertaking. Faith and religion, on the other hand, are above all matters of feeling in which ultimately the faithful heart remains the highest authority. Also in the realm of the eternally incomplete search for the truth, which does not have to be a monopoly of reason.

RAHNER:
Yes, good. But even if I am convinced that one must silently and worshipfully dismiss all statements about God into the incomprehensibility of God, then it still does not follow for me that all statements that people make about God are equal. One is right (let's leave the word *true* alone) and the other is simply false and not equal. You and I must maintain the courage to make such a distinction, even though we know that everything we say about God stands under the proviso about the incomprehensibility of God, that (as the Fourth Lateran Council of 1215 said) no similarity between God

and us can be predicated, and that a still greater dissimilarity between us and God must be predicated.

LAPIDE:
In the Bible, which I believe remains our fundamental document of faith, practically everything about their experiences of God was written down initially by divinely inspired people in the luminosity of those experiences. Only much later was it read and explained dispassionately and cerebrally by cold-blooded academics. I fear that much of the original treasure of faith has fallen victim to this "change of climate." For what is written in burning devotion and with passionate love may contradict itself a hundred times over without diminishing its profound truth-content in the least. For here it concerns truth that pure reason cannot discern. In the words of Blaise Pascal, the heart has its reasons which reason knows not.

RAHNER:
I would be more careful and not so quickly see head and heart, reason and love as simple opposites. Also I would not ascribe to love a language that may contradict itself a hundred times over. The statement "Auschwitz was a horrible crime" and the statement "Auschwitz belongs to the ordinary activity of human history" are not statements that permit themselves to be integrated into the language of love or even into the language of the head. The first sentence is true and the other sentence is false and a vulgarity. So also with theological statements which, as much as they must be consigned as it were to

the mystery of God, are true and correct or, on the other hand, are false. If one said, "there are hundreds of gods," you would certainly not say that is a valid statement simply because it is the language of love.

LOGIC AND HUMILITY

LAPIDE:
I would distinguish here between two categories of
thought: the antirational, which I reject since God en-
dowed me with reason in order to test, to think, and to
decide. Opposite this stands the supernatural, which
neither offends my reason nor gives it the lie, although
it stands head and shoulders above it. In other words, I
am not prepared to say with Tertullian: I believe because it is absurd. For that means leaving my reason in
the cloak room of the synagogue before I enter the sanc-
tuary. Contrary to this, I agree with Prince Hamlet,
who rightly asserts, there are more things in heaven and
earth than are dreamt of in our philosophy.

Nonsense about God is absurd; paradox here and
there may belong to the mystics, but multiplicity of
meaning, even if it appears irrational, may very well be
valid as a genuine expression of faith. For instance,
when in the Hebrew Bible God is called judge and ac-
cuser, witness and interrogator, righteous and merciful,
jealous and totally long-suffering, one can place these
statements neither on the scale of reason nor under the
microscope of logic, for both would be instantly ex-

posed as ostensible self-contradictions. In the language of the love of God, though, they not only have their own depth of meaning but also possess a strong power of expression. The language of true faith resembles the language of love in so many respects. What the groom has to say to his bride may be poor logic; it is, however, always splendid cardio-logic. The same obtains also for the theo-logic of the heart's piety.

RAHNER:
Good. I can agree with that. Only I would add that my intellect itself can observe that a person may speak and must speak beyond mere rationality, and such speech therefore does not, in the sense of an absolute irrationalism, simply exist unmediated beside rational speech.

LAPIDE:
Agreed.

RAHNER:
But there is still more. I cannot incorporate everything into the language of rationalistic logic. But with my rationality I can appreciate that I must not and should not do that at all. This insight, however, is still very important for me.

LAPIDE:
Logic is a superior organ of our humanity, but it should learn humility. For as soon as reason fancies itself to be the supreme judge of the true and false, good and evil, it falls into delusions of grandeur and no longer serves the

name of reason. The discreet recognition of its own boundaries belongs to the essence of reason.

RAHNER:
Logic should appreciate that this humility belongs to proper logic itself.

LAPIDE:
Therefore: a logic of the heart.

RAHNER:
No. For me human rationality only reaches its apex when it rejects as a false pretension the notion of itself as a final authority, and realizes that it must do so according to its own principles.

LAPIDE:
Have you never suffered a conflict between your head and your heart?

RAHNER:
I don't actually know whether my head has been so impudent as to pose as the highest authority in such a conflict. But naturally it is always possible that something like this can happen in individual instances without one noticing it.

LAPIDE:
Perhaps all genuine faith is a golden mean between the heart and the head. Both should possess equal rights of codetermination—without pretensions of being able to monopolize. With the possible exception of the mystics,

who obey their own system of laws. Mysticism comes from *myein*, closing the eyes (and ears) in order to better see and hear inwardly. But most mystics do not hold their tongues—to our benefit. For example, someone like Meister Eckhart.

RAHNER:

My friend Heribert Fischer, a prominent Eckhart specialist, has argued that if Eckhart was a mystic in the true sense of the word, he would naturally only have been a highly meditative and radically speculative theologian. But we should not argue about this now.

LAPIDE:

Let's take as an example John of the Cross, who had Jewish blood in his veins. And Theresa of Avila, who not only descended from Jews but also—consciously or unconsciously—used Jewish concepts in her writings. Spain was certainly at one time the home of Jewish and Christian mysticism, with reciprocal cross-communication and cross-fertilization that still awaits the researcher.

RAHNER:

You know of course that the founder of my order, Ignatius Loyola, gladly acknowledged being of Jewish descent (he said that three times, if I remember correctly), though he was thoroughly Basque.

LAPIDE:

Why then did your order only repeal its notorious "Aryan clause" at the end of 1946?

RAHNER:
I truly don't know.

LAPIDE:
That should not be an accusation; only a sad look back at an unfortunate past.

RAHNER:
In the history of every great institution there are stupidities, erroneous decisions, terrible things. In my case one must say either that the order itself was guilty of a cowardly, erroneous decision in deplorably and reprehensibly capitulating before the anti-Semitism in Spain at the time, or that it had legitimate reasons not to circumvent this Aryan clause, in order to be able to continue its work unhindered. Put a bit nastily, if in earlier times a baptized Jew could not become a Jesuit, then not very much was denied him.

LAPIDE:
We should not forget that Lainez and Polanco, Ignatius's best friends, were both half-Jewish. But what did Ignatius intend to say when he said that he longed to be descended from the flesh and blood of Jesus?

RAHNER:
Probably in Ignatius's case that was a reaction, inspired by the love of Jesus, against the prevailing anti-Semitism, especially in Spain. What else could it have been? It is not so easy even for a Jesuit today to understand why Ignatius was initially so absolute in wanting to live

permanently in Palestine and was dissuaded from this only through the force of external circumstances. Naturally you could say that he wanted to convert the Jews there. But there were hardly any left. So, what then did Ignatius really want in Palestine? That he just wanted to convert the Muslims is also not so apparent to me. He was simply interested, intensively so, in the fully concrete Jesus—more than contemporary theology, which contemplates the Incarnation and the hypostatic union and is actually little interested in the concreteness of Jesus.

THE JEWISHNESS
OF JESUS

LAPIDE:

Today post-Easter Christology receives more than its due, often to the disadvantage of the earthly Jesus of Nazareth.

RAHNER:

That Jesus was human, lived and died, precisely in Palestine and Jerusalem, preoccupied the love of Ignatius for Jesus in a most intensive way. For example, it was a fundamental matter of existential concern for Ignatius that he wanted to be as poor as Jesus and that his order should also remain true to the poverty of Jesus. The later Jesuits have certainly affirmed this in theory, but in practice (if even on understandable grounds), they have not taken it with complete seriousness. So Ignatius was probably more interested in the Jewishness of Jesus than we average Christians today.

LAPIDE:

Does this attitude of your founder not attest to a profoundly serious regard for the Incarnation? In the sense of Karl Barth, who wrote: "The meaning can also not be that we believe in Jesus Christ who now was an Israelite by chance, but who could just as well also be descended from another race. Here one must think with total rigor: Jesus Christ . . . was necessarily Jewish. . . . God became human in Jewish flesh. This fact is not to be overlooked, for it belongs to the concrete actuality of God and his revelation." Accordingly, the Jewishness of Jesus is not abstractable from the Incarnation.

RAHNER:

Naturally you must concede to me that I have the right to say that whether Jesus had black or blond hair, wore a beard or not, is inconsequential for me in the final analysis. There are even realities about Jesus as the redeemer and savior, as the center and climax of salvation history, that can be of no concern to a Christian in his or her religious theory and practice. There are certain other historically contingent things about Jesus that one cannot deduce from an abstract idea of the Incarnation and that are nevertheless of religious significance for a Christian. Like, for example, the fact for Ignatius that Jesus was poor. So also today many Christians and followers of Jesus will say that it is of fundamental significance that Jesus did not stand on the side of the capitalists but rather on the side of the poor and oppressed. From there one can naturally ask whether the Jewishness of Jesus belongs above all to the aforementioned contingent characteristics of Jesus or whether as such it has a specific religious significance for us Christians— and what this is if the Jewishness of Jesus must be understood in this second sense.

LAPIDE:

The declaration of the German bishops of 28 April 1980, "On the Relationship of the Church to Judaism," begins with the following sentence: "Whoever encounters Jesus Christ encounters Judaism." This is a statement that the pope also made his own when he spoke to a Jewish delegation in Mainz in November 1980. That is *not* to say, "encounters the elitist Judaism, a partial Judaism, or an original Judaism," but rather simply and plainly "encounters Judaism." Subsequently the statement of the bishops places in the middle of an eightfold list the assertion that the Jewishness of Jesus in no way exhausts itself in his biological flesh and blood, but rather manifests itself especially in his spiritual world and in the richness of his faith. All this has nothing to do with the length of his beard and his skin color, but rather belongs to the quintessence of his human existence.

RAHNER:

There above all I must register a difficulty in understanding. If they say, for instance, that Jesus was just, that Jesus regarded men and women equally, then if I am a Christian I can naturally say that these attitudes, which he in fact ultimately got from his Jewish tradition, are obviously binding for Christians too. However at least many such attitudes of Jesus, which were for him actually Jewish and which are binding even for me, are nevertheless basically general human self-understandings. Perhaps they were preached in a grand manner in the Judaism of the period before Jesus and were naturally also realized by Jesus himself, but the Jewish origin in Jesus is of no interest for Christians today. The authentic question is still: Did Jesus preach and live normative attitudes that are valid for us today, attitudes that can be deduced neither from abstract, constant, general human nature nor from the Incarnation, and yet are still binding for Christians? For example, is an "option" for the poor and underprivileged, in distinction to general, valid "natural-law" norms, a binding norm for Christians according to Jesus? And also the reverse, are there modes of behavior that were Jesus' that cannot be deduced from the most general premises and are nevertheless obligatory for a Christian? I myself would certainly not venture to speak against opponents in religious questions in the way Jesus did against the Pharisees, as far as his words have been transmitted.

LAPIDE:

Assuming that I could provide you with convincing proof that the Lord's Prayer amounted to a shortened version of the synagogue liturgy, that the entire Sermon on the Mount along with the admonition to love one's enemies developed from rabbinical constructions, that virtually all the parables of Jesus achieve their full measure of meaning only from their Jewish background—and if I could add to this evidence that the Gospel writers frequently misunderstood their master and erroneously translated him into Greek because they did not have command of his Semitic mother tongue, would you then be prepared to concede that Jesus' spiritual Jewishness must count as an indispensable component of Christology?

RAHNER:
Yes, I can concede that the Jewish spiritual world at the time of Jesus is of indispensable significance. However, it remains true nevertheless that there are also historical conditions in Jesus that need not be normative for a Christian.

LAPIDE:
Certainly. No person can demand that one become an imitator of Jesus in regard to all customs and habits. But perhaps Christians should think and believe in a more Jesus-like way and somewhat less in a Pauline way.

RAHNER:
If I could express myself a bit more generally for a moment, I would say that in his polemics Paul is often simply un-Christian.

LAPIDE:
I am ready to forgive him for his polemics, which often border on rabid crudity. In the final analysis, he had numerous opponents—as many in Judaism as in early Christianity—and in the heat of verbal combat something would not infrequently slip out that he probably would rather have left unsaid. Also, his borrowings from Greek philosophy and his Jewish-Hellenistic intermingling are still somehow understandable. Here and there, it appears to me that he knowingly distorted biblical quotations, altered written words and intentionally called things by incorrect names. He himself said he wanted to be a Jew to the Jews and a Greek to

the Greeks—perhaps even a proverbial Jesuit to the Jesuits, for whom the end justifies the means.

RAHNER:
We Jesuits have never taught that.

LAPIDE:
I realize that, although countless rumors continue to persist about that. Still, all joking aside, if you deem the Jewishness of the person of Jesus unimportant or theologically irrelevant, then fundamentally you commit the error of "deincarnation"—the reduction of a living human figure to an abstract, bodiless idea.

RAHNER:
Yes, but my question is still not answered thereby. As a Jew you cannot deny, in spite of all the chosenness of the Jews, that you and I are two people who simply on the basis of our common humanity have reciprocal obligations. And so I can also still maintain that in Jesus such humanity was a given, which, preceding his Jewishness, can be normative for me, and that he offered declarations and challenges out of this common humanity that are significant for us.

LAPIDE:
Granted.

RAHNER:
Now that is one side of the problem. There is, however, also another side. Most probably you will not argue with me if I say that Jesus wore headgear that is not

obligatory for me. (I name one arbitrary example from among many other imaginable ones.) How do I distinguish between these two aspects of the reality of Jesus? The question is very difficult for me because I cannot contend from the outset that my relationship to Jesus can be codetermined by realities and predicates of his that are not identical to his universal human nature and the predicates based thereupon. But there are still also realities and predicates of his that are not normative for me—for example, like a piece of headgear, like a skullcap.

LAPIDE:

We can do without your skullcap—although the pope wears one.

RAHNER:

Does that come from the Jews?

LAPIDE:

I don't know for sure, but because the Vatican and the whole body of cardinals of the Curia, who also wear skullcaps, received so much from the religious world of Israel, perhaps the skullcap is also part of the Jewish bequest to the Church. It serves as a symbol of respect and it provides a distinction between heaven (the residence of God) and my head. Moreover, in antiquity bareheadedness was thought of as a mark of freedom, while slaves and helots had to wear a type of hood. With his headcovering the Jew intended to say that he was a servant of God who had voluntarily taken the yoke of the kingdom of heaven upon himself. However that may be, you as a Christian need neither to cover your head nor to eat kosher, but you should nevertheless adhere to the accords of the apostolic councils—and every believing Christian should do that. It has to do with those so-called seven commands of Noah's sons (Acts 15:19–29) that present a type of elementary ethic and whose non-Jewish followers were honored by the authoritative rabbis as "the righteous people of the world," who have "a share in the world to come." However, Jesus—whom the Gospel writers (not just by chance) deem "Rabbi" on eleven occasions—maintained all 613 of the commands and prohibitions of Judaism that are obligatory only for religious Jews.

RAHNER:
But nevertheless you must put on a skullcap and I don't need to. It has to do with your Jewishness and it doesn't have anything to do with me.

LAPIDE:
Agreed.

RAHNER:
That means, though, that in the Jewishness of Jesus I may once more distinguish, and must distinguish, between what simply belongs to this Jewishness and what is normative therein for me as a Gentile Christian.

ADDITIONS, NOT HEIRS

LAPIDE:

Correct. But then you must regard yourself as "being an addition," as "incorporated" into the covenant people, as "co-citizens, co-heirs, and co-partakers of the promise," as Paul calls you (Eph. 2:19; 3:6), but not as successor, usurper, expropriator, or even as heir of a still vital Israel. One can only be an heir, according to *Duden*,[6] to someone who is already dead. In short, you should take Ephesians 2 somewhat more seriously.

RAHNER:

It is not so obvious to me whether one must understand this being an addition to a still vital Israel in precisely the way you have just explained it.

LAPIDE:

It is remarkable how many descriptive terms for Gentile Christians Paul coined, all of which begin with the prefix *co*—co-heirs, co-citizens, co-incorporated, co-redeemed, co-partakers, etc. Words that taken together indicate that the olive tree of Israel with its old root stock

6. German dictionary.—TRANS.

still "supports" the Church as later "grafted branches" (Rom. 11:16–24) and these new branches could not dispense with the nourishing roots without withering up. Both should understand themselves as equal limbs in and of the same tree of faith that complement each other organically through their distinctiveness. Since according to Paul a close connection exists between Christ and Torah (law), one should reflect anew upon this duality in light of his total corpus. God's "holy, just, and good law" (Rom. 7:12), in which even the apostle to the Gentiles "delights" (Rom. 7:22), was, according to Paul, given only to the people of Israel—after the covenant and promise had been given to them, which were and are the basis and ground of the continually valid Torah. If there is no "law" without covenant and promise, then it is just as senseless to force the law upon those Gentile Christians who are "strangers to the covenants of promise" (Eph. 2:12), as it would be superfluous to force Christ upon the Jews—those Jews who remain post-Easter members of the people of God and covenant partners of God (Rom. 9:4 and 11:29), and who are certain of the final salvation (Rom. 11:26). That Jesus became savior to the Gentiles even without being the Messiah of Israel must in no way be a contradiction, unless we insist upon stuffing God's "manifold wisdom" (Eph. 3:10) and his "varied grace" (1 Pet. 4:10) into a narrow black-and-white scheme that only knows a single either-or: either baptized or damned. Shouldn't we finally credit God with more imagination than the exclusivity of a single one-way street leading to his salvation? I don't want to put a yarmulke on you and you wouldn't force a mass upon me, for I believe with Jesus that "in my Father's house are many rooms" (Jn. 14:2) into which leads an entire network of streets, roads, and paths. "We are all God's co-workers," Paul says correctly (1 Cor. 3:9), whereby everyone so serves as the Lord assigned to each (1 Cor. 3:5). And then it states, still clearer and in a more rabbinical vein, on the next pages of his first Letter to the Corinthians: "Was any one at the time of his call already circumcised? Let him not seek to remove the marks of the circumcision. Was any one at the time of his call uncircumcised? Let him not seek circumcision. For neither circumcision counts for anything nor uncircumcision, but keeping the commandments of God" (1 Cor. 7:18–19).

That the Jew Jesus binds us together as well as separates us, that he is a bridge as well as a barrier—this ambivalence should serve as food for thought in order for us to ponder dialogically the inscrutability of the way of God.

RAHNER:

For me all you said about the way of Israel to God comes down to the final decisive question of whether Jesus is also the redeemer of the Jews and is recognized as such by them. According to the presupposition of this recognition, I could then, as a Gentile Christian theologian, still ask whether, and in what sense, I can recognize a particular way of Israel in distinction to the way of us Gentile Christians.

SPEAKING THE TRUTH
IN LOVE

***

LAPIDE:

When I sit with you like this, I am overcome for a moment by the feeling of the all-encompassing fellowship of God. The centuries of alienation dissolve, and two sons of one father sit across from one another—two sons who have seriously argued and drifted apart, but who finally come to the insight that the fatherly benefaction envelops them both. Gradually it dawns upon them that this contending among themselves may admittedly have thousands of humanly valid reasons, but nevertheless does not accord with the redemptive intentions of their common creator. Such an overview can scarcely harm our dialogue.

RAHNER:

Naturally I am basically in agreement with the description you have given of our mutual relationship. But that still doesn't change the fact that presumably there are fundamental religious and ideological differences between us that we cannot simply pass over. Whether a deeper unity lies hidden behind these religious differences (which must be taken seriously)—and how one interprets it—is still another question. In any case, we are simply not yet united in what we will probably say to one another. We can therefore only postulate in hope that behind that in which we are not united there is nevertheless a fundamental unity. But despite the hope at this level, about which we can speak with one another with human words, we must take the religious differences seriously.

LAPIDE:

So seriously that none of us should renounce one iota of his religious position. The dialogue frequently doesn't concern the faith itself, but the angle of vision, the way of seeing, and the manner of articulation. In all these modalities the motto of Pope John XXIII hovers before me: *veritas in caritate.* We owe each other the truth—but in love.

RAHNER:

After all, *alētheuein en agapē* ("speak the truth in love") is already found in Paul.

LAPIDE:

In accepting the Reuchlin Prize of the City of Pforzheim in 1965, you said: "A Christian will conduct the dialogue earnestly in the knowledge of the danger that within himself the sin of pride, of stubbornness, of false self-security, of brutality poisons the dialogue and causes social lies. . . . The Christian knows . . . that one must be able to say of his dialogue what the apostle said of love: In true dialogue one is patient, kind, not jealous, one does not boast, one is not arrogant, one does not insist upon one's own way, one does not play the hypocrite, one does not become resentful, one does not resent the evil suffered, one hopes all things, one endures all things, for one knows—even in the conviction of one's own truth—that one still sees as in a mirror dimly and in part." I could wish for no better guiding word for a Christian-Jewish religious dialogue.

RAHNER:

I hope that in the present dialogue between us this description of a true dialogue is not denied. One never knows for sure reflexively whether this description is being lived up to or not. For on the one hand, one must represent a definite, clear conviction in the face of one's dialogue partner who is of another conviction. And on the other hand, one should do so precisely in the manner just described. To unite both, though, is difficult, and whether one actually brings it off always remains unclear.

LAPIDE:

When I endeavor to survey the entire terrain of the Christian-Jewish discussion *sub specie aeternitatis*—all two millennia of divergence—it appears to me that from an initial brotherly argument developed a still fruitful rivalry ("a struggle over heaven") that all too quickly dissolved into opposition and finally degenerated into hostility. In Buber's German one could say: from *Be-gegnung* (encounter) came *Ent-gegnung* (objection), then *Ver-gegnung* (reprisal) and finally destructive *Zer-gegnung* (antagonism). Is it not time for us to ask ourselves the basic question: Where is HE, our Father in heaven, who separates and divides us? What has alienated Jews and Christians for such a long time? And where are we, with our handiwork and our human faculties, erecting the walls that put barriers in the way and prevent an actual coming together?

RAHNER:

I believe one must make a distinction between two questions: On the level of what can be expressed, can one come to an agreement through the dialogue described above? And what do I accept as already given in the dialogue partner, then and there, when this desired agreement is not yet given on the level of what can be expressed?

THE "OPEN" REVELATION

LAPIDE:

The three main branches of the Reformation—Lutheran, Calvinist, and United, which in religious matters had bickered destructively for a century—reached agreement in the Leuenberger Concordat that none of their differences should be ignored or annulled, but neither should they be perceived any more as "schismatic." Could one not say, *mutatis mutandis*, that Christian and Jewish convictions, as they have crystallized in the course of the centuries, should stand as they are? But that at the same time we grant absolute priority to the first things: namely, the common love of God, love of neighbor as the touchstone of faith, the hope of salvation, and our unshakable expectation of a total redemption that makes the future God's greatest dimension. Could one not say that these cardinal common elements create a minimal basis of consensus for an initial biblical ecumenicity of Jews and Christians?

RAHNER:

I must express myself with care and say the following with the reservation that I can still reflect upon it later myself. The Jew who accepts the Old Testament as binding revelation and we Christians and Catholics who do the same naturally do not have the same relationship as that which exists between the various Christian confessions when these make mutually contradictory statements about the meaning of Christian revelation. The Catholic still maintains the conviction that he, to be sure, says something very essential beyond the Old Testament, in a certain sense something downright fundamentally essential. But he does not need to challenge what you recognize as the divine revelation of the Old Testament. Certainly, insofar as the Jew considers his Old Testament revelation definitive and no longer surpassable and not decisively continued in Jesus of Nazareth, there exists then in this perspective a more fundamental difference between Jews and Christians than between the individual Christian confessions that all recognize Jesus as their Lord and Savior.

LAPIDE:

What could help us further perhaps is the fact that both the Hebrew Bible and the New Testament are open books. Only the written canon is closed, but their message is open and communicates in a threefold manner: open above to the sovereign salvific will of God, open ahead to God's future that none of us is privileged to have prior knowledge of, and open on all sides to the people of the world to whose service we are both called. Two examples may clarify this. Malachi, one of the last prophets, closes his book with the prophecy: "Behold, I will send you Elijah the prophet before the great and terrible day of the Lord comes" (Mal. 4:5).

In his farewell speech to his disciples, Jesus said: "I have yet many things to say to you, but you cannot bear them now. When the Spirit of truth comes, he will guide you into all the truth. . . . He will declare to you the things that are to come" (Jn. 16:12–13). The final word of God is therefore not yet spoken; a future revelation for us both has still not yet arrived. Jews and Christians should therefore know not only about their own imperfection but also about the open-endedness of salvation history and the incompleteness of our world. With Paul, I would even take a further step and say that "the sufferings of this present time are not worth comparing with the glory that is to be revealed to us" (Rom. 8:18). In other words, the most beautiful and the greatest that God wants to give us lies still before us as a treasure of hope that can already brighten even our present with its rays. If, however, that coming fulfillment will cause all our previous experiences of redemption to pale—as Paul, Peter, and the rabbis believe—would that not be ground enough to shift the emphasis of our doctrine of salvation to that lodestar of security, whose advent we could still live to see, as God wishes?

RAHNER:
I believe I must distinguish sharply here. That the self-understanding of Judaism and also that of Christianity remains open to the future in a true sense, and that the Christian understanding of the revelation given in Jesus Christ still stands in history and so is not completed, are obvious to me. However now I must add the following: the absolute future for me is not something that takes place within history during the course of history; rather

it is what takes place in my death and for the world as a whole in its fulfillment that concludes history. It is also obvious that in this arrival of the absolute future, in my and the world's fulfillment in the immediacy of God "face to face," everything that I stammer here on earth as a poor Christian theologian will be radically surpassed. Inasmuch as my radical fulfillment in the immediacy of God and that of the world is irrevocably promised me, and consequently the absoluteness of the truth of the perception of God in Jesus Christ, this promise can in actuality not be superseded, but rather has already itself superseded all possible and conceivable inner-worldly, and also religious, futures.

I don't doubt that by the year 3000, if humanity still exists, much will have been additionally acquired in the way of inner-worldly spiritual knowledge. However, in any case, it falls short of the absolute truth promised the person in the perception of God in Jesus Christ and so doesn't interest me so terribly, especially since I will have already "been long gone."

ADVENT OR RETURN
OF THE MESSIAH?

LAPIDE:

Me, too—into the kingdom of eternal truth, as I hope. However, here below we are in between both "victims" of the so-called delay of the parousia (which in Greek stands for "advent"). For over two thousand years the Synagogue has prayed for the advent of the Messiah and for around nineteen hundred years the Church has prayed for the return of its redeemer. Unfortunately, our intercessions have remained unfulfilled to this day.

RAHNER:

You will permit me to observe in advance that I do not regard the concept of "return" very auspiciously. For instance, when one returns then the old is still there. The parousia of Jesus, which we pray and hope for and have not yet experienced, however, is not simply the restitution of the situation in which we live and in which Jesus once lived.

LAPIDE:

I can carry that further. However, how do you understand that place in the Acts of the Apostles where after the ascension two angels indicate to the apostles that Jesus will return "in the same way as he was taken up"? The Greek text permits one to assume that his return will occur in the same manner as his departure into heaven took place.

RAHNER:
Thus the meaning of this text is obscure, I think.

LAPIDE:
The word *houtōs*, though, signifies: in the same manner, just as—which suggests under comparable circumstances.

RAHNER:
Still, that only says that this Jesus is the same as the one in whom is given the irrevocable promise of God, in which God himself is promised to us as our absolute future.

LAPIDE:
You may be right, inasmuch as the future remains *terra incognita.* Various commentators infer from Acts 1:11 that Jesus' parousia on the Mount of Olives, expected in the midst of a Jewish Jerusalem, corresponds to the circumstances of his ascension.

RAHNER:
Now, I am happy to be a rationalist, who still regards himself as such and places his rationality in question. I don't mean thereby that Jesus must return on the clouds of heaven, clad in some particular raiment, at the end of

time. That is an image that must be translated. Here one may "demythologize" a little. These New Testament images are images that naturally have an inexpressible content that remains in force, but can also basically be expressed without these images. The content, not the image itself as such, belongs to the obligatory faith of Catholic theologians.

LAPIDE:

Here also I am in agreement with you. Figurative language is certainly not to be taken literally at all. It is still true that Jews and Christians have hoped for a long time now for the coming of the final redeemer—but so far in vain. What is the meaning then of the plea "Thy kingdom come!" in the Lord's Prayer, to which there is a Jewish parallel in our daily liturgy, if not the eloquent expression of the unquenchable yearning for redemption?

RAHNER:

Naturally. But also viewed historically, the early Christians regarded the parousia as a temporally imminent expectation, not as an absolute, binding doctrine of faith, because they knew that the actual day of the Lord was known only to the Father himself. They were disappointed by the vision that they nurtured of the parousia of God in Jesus Christ, in which they believed and which they still found valid. But behind and underneath this disappointment, still for you and me, one hopes, there is an expectation that is not disappointing and will not be disappointing.

LAPIDE:

In fact, as far as perseverance is concerned, we could both point to outstanding accomplishments. Jews are a tad ahead of you, for we have already prayed for over two thousand years for the messianic redemption. You have done so for about nineteen hundred years. We should share the world's record for the ability to hope together as brothers, for I know of no third religion that, in spite of all disappointments and delays, has manifested such unshakable certainty of salvation—and continues to testify further to it.

RAHNER:

I must stress once again: I hope for the final self-communication of God face to face. For me, that is the absolute future. That alone. Then the incomprehensible God, whom I cannot grasp absolutely, will be given as such. But then I will finally be accepted by him. What still transpires for me in the earthly, temporal, and historical future in which I die before long and what transpires for earthly humanity in its history, one can wish for oneself in various ways. One can hope and expect that in this interim time still many others will become better and grander. Yes, one must by all means say that the work of betterment of this interim temporal future is the essential condition for the person's actually obtaining by God's grace the absolute future that is God himself. But somehow these intermediate stations, if I may call them that, between today and the absolute future that is God himself as such are in a certain sense not so important and interesting to me. Everyone, therefore myself included, must make the effort to see that this interim time supports more in the way of human self-realization than already exists. But if the consequence of such effort does not produce something especially wonderful, then this still requires the patience and perseverance you spoke of. And Christians may not allow themselves to be shaken ultimately in this effort, which is surely demanded of them, as a result of very modest successes and many failures.

LAPIDE:
Didn't you say somewhere in your *Foundations of Faith* that for you the definitive self-communication of God happened in Jesus Christ?

RAHNER:
I fear I am being misunderstood.

LAPIDE:
Perhaps I did not perceive you correctly there. It appeared to me that according to your view the God of Abraham, Isaac, and Jacob had manifested himself definitively in Jesus Christ.

RAHNER:
No. I must say: in Jesus is given to me the irrevocable promise of the definitive self-communication of God. I still await this self-communication itself, even if, as Paul says, the "earnest money" for it is already given to me in grace.

THE COMMON HOPE

LAPIDE:

I am happy to have strayed here. For the divine self-revelation, "I AM WHO I AM" (Ex. 3:14), affirms in the rabbinical explanation also that no one is permitted to anticipate or know in advance the forms of God's appearance. Still less is it possible to claim to determine what God will do in the future or will allow.

RAHNER:

I don't know what God still plans for us within this worldly time. However, if I state my hopeful belief that God desires to give himself in his own most particular reality and splendor to me, then I still have the right to say: there can be nothing beyond that in all eternity because there is nothing beyond God himself. And this God communicates himself to me as my fulfillment and not simply as a creative, finite gift.

LAPIDE:

I certainly would not want to contradict a thing. However, beyond God himself I may not forget his world, for which we have been made responsible. This earthly unredemptiveness, under which "the whole creation has been groaning in travail together until now" (Rom. 8:22), is for me an indication that God's promises are not yet fulfilled and his love story with humanity still has a long way to go to reach its goal.

RAHNER:
The promise of God to give himself directly to us in his own most particular reality is for those of us who still dwell here not yet fulfilled. As I have already said, this God, who as himself is our absolute future, desires that this earthly temporality, which in Jesus Christ belongs to his own biography, become better than it is now. Thus I can naturally also say that there are particular historical, social, and individual biographical lacunae in this story, whose resolution I must still hope for.

LAPIDE:
Faithful Jews do the same. Then incorrigible optimists about redemption like Karl Rahner, Pinchas Lapide, and many million of like-minded people could found an alliance of hope that would publicly proclaim that a better future on this earth and for its total inhabitants, as an interim station on our way to the end time, is our heart's concern and our coresponsibility—while the absolute future of fulfillment lies in God's hand. Would that not be a further piece of common interest?

RAHNER:
To be sure. In this secularizing darkness, malaise, and banality, amidst an organized and institutionalized atheism, everyone who believes in the eternal, holy, immeasurable God, who is the God of Abraham, Isaac, and

Jesus, should together with the Muslims be conscious that they have a common interest vis-à-vis this world that's left that they should and could take much more seriously. Of course I would still say that I interpret many so-called atheists as theists who do not yet understand themselves in their own true essence of freedom.

LAPIDE:

Many atheists reveal themselves upon closer examination as anticlerical or as pseudoatheists who are perplexed by the small gnomelike God palmed off on them at school or at home. However, they are all, as you once said, "troubled atheists," who are intensely distressed by the absence of God and care passionately about our world. For atheists, the concern of the faithful for God sounds like a camouflaged concern for the world, while the pain many atheists experience over the world and the fate of our earth equates to a disguised, often unconscious concern for God. Only the apathetic and the indifferent, for whom everything is all the same and accordingly irrelevant, are unconcerned. I don't fear the genuine atheists who say no to God for the sake of humanity, but rather those uncaring ones who yawn in God's face because the God-question no longer holds any meaning for them.

RAHNER:

Quite right. The state atheism in communist countries and the atheism in the public life of the West have one thing in common: lack of interest in the God-question, absorption into the banality of our world. Both are equally horrible and dreary. However, the troubled atheist, who suffers over the world, who is in solidarity with the underprivileged, and who says there couldn't be a God because of the horribleness of this world—I am thoroughly sympathetic with this person. The banal philistine atheism, which exists in Russian state religion and with us, even if not as an official state doctrine but in practice all the same, is surely our true common enemy.

LAPIDE:

If you conducted an extensive debate with some Jewish atheists, it would frequently come out that they are basically antitheistic: angry at God because, according to their view, he allowed one-and-a-half-million Jewish children to burn. What most of them don't know is that in their indignation they maintain the faith of one of the oldest Jewish traditions. They contend with their creator as Abraham once did over Sodom and Gomorrha; they petition like Jeremiah; they demand an accounting like Job and wrangle with him as our ancestor Jacob once did at the ford of the Jabbok. Israel (the new name that Jacob was able to wrest from God in that combative night) signifies "He who strives with God"— a characteristic which Father Jacob, together with the new name, bequeathed to his entire posterity. That nevertheless has nothing to do with atheism, for only an insane person battles something or someone whose existence he denies. The Jewish striving with God is perhaps the highest level of the acknowledgment of God— a profound, relentless, serious acceptance of the Lord of the world who will endure no injustice, no stain on the image of God.

RAHNER:

By and large, I agree with that completely. As a philosopher (which I am not), though, I would still add the following: that in some sense there is an absolute, a final basis, and a final unity of the world that, in my opinion, a reasonable person cannot essentially deny. The holy Improbable (which is difficult for me and all people) consists of the fact that despite human finitude and particularity one can still have dealings with this Absolute, that one can address him as "you," that one can pray, and that despite his absoluteness (out of which he exploded the world millions of light years ago) he is *my* God. The trusting, personal, loving relationship to the Absolute—who cannot be less a person than I myself am, who knows about himself and me—is the characteristic feature of Christianity in distinction to an Asian mysticism of dissolution according to which one must, in a manner of speaking, fall into the absolute abyss of nothingness. We Christians believe in the unutterable absoluteness of God, which nevertheless manages to reach us in order to say yes to us. For me, a mysticism of a personal God, properly understood, is not lower than a mysticism of an impersonal Absolute but higher, because the former transcends the all too human elements of the latter, elements that actually annihilate the human.

LAPIDE:

I cannot do much with divinity as prototype, as all-knowing, as ground of all being, or as "the wholly other." HE is for me not a God of logic, but of dialogue:

the intimate "you," to whom I can say Father, pour out my heart, and know in my deepest self that I am carried and guided by a higher power who enables me to love and be open to faith. It is the unbelievable security in the hiddenness of God, the wholly illogical but unshakable certainty of an intimate togetherness that makes all the misery of humanity bearable, permits me to cope and persevere, and fills my heart with unspeakable thanksgiving.

Godless people (assuming there are any) appear to me to be metaphysically handicapped, for the most human of all dimensions is lacking to them: the sense of the personal God. Those pseudoatheists who seek God in humanism have simply lost patience with salvation. Thus they renounce God's assistance and expend all their energy in so-called self-redemption, which often is nothing other than unconscious cooperation with God's redemptive work. We religious people, in contrast, have more endurance. Even when he hems and haws from out of his unfathomable reasons, he will still finally redeem us, for "God is faithful" (1 Cor. 1:9). He stands by his promises.

RAHNER:

Only parenthetically and quite modestly, I would add to your justifiable rejection of my ability to redeem myself the following. In a session with Buddhists in Vienna, I once said that I cannot actually admit that the alternative between self-redemption and redemption by another is final. I simply cannot do this because this God who redeems us does so out of the innermost center of our own reality so that in a certain sense we do this ourselves. We love God with the power that is God himself.

LAPIDE:
The Hasidim underscored a similar line of reasoning in their double slogan: do good, as if there were no God and everything depended upon you—but at the same time pray as if everything depends upon God!

RAHNER:
Ignatius Loyola formulated it in almost precisely the same way.

LAPIDE:
It's remarkable how the giants nod to one another. In patristics and in the works of the high scholastics, I often bumped into insights and concepts that had almost verbatim analogies in the Talmud. These affinities should also be discussed sometime. But back to the common hope: the Church prays daily for the parousia of Christ, the synagogue for the arrival of the Messiah. Because there can only be one single and universal bringer of salvation according to Christian soteriology as well as in Jewish teaching about the Messiah, so the fervent expectation must be for our common redeemer. That he will be Jesus of Nazareth is a certainty for you and a not-to-be-precluded possibility for me. No more, but also no less. So here therefore there is no Jewish no standing over against a Christian yes, but rather a Christian yes to a humble Jewish question mark.

RAHNER:

We are then certainly very close. Whether one is true in his conscience before God or not is something that no one can know with reflexive certainty. But when and where a person actually follows his conscience, then and there he is certainly at peace with God. If you therefore say: as a Jew I have a humble question mark about Jesus and we both hope together for an ultimate redemption, then based on my normal Catholic faith and the Second Vatican Council, I have no reason to doubt that in spite of the differences in our relationship to Jesus we meet in a radical decision for the good and so reach the one and the same God.

LAPIDE:

I would like to venture the following summary. Christians and Jews have a common beginning in biblical Israel; they await one and the same resolution as fulfillment of the promises; and the ethos of the Bible and the predictions of the prophets illumine their steps on the path of this pilgrimage to the end-time. These four fundamental common elements could be the supporting pillars of Christian-Jewish ecumenism.

RAHNER:

Certainly. Only you may not in principle deny me my right to my hope that you as a Jew will recognize one day (when, naturally, I don't know) that Jesus, your brother "according to the flesh," is the unsurpassable and irrevocable promise, or the one whose glorification by God is for the sake of the promises that God himself gave Israel and finally also us Gentiles.

THE ROLE OF JESUS
IN GOD'S PLAN
OF SALVATION

LAPIDE:

That Jesus had a central role to fulfill in the divine plan of salvation (which is largely unknown to me) through which the West has been led to faith in the one God in his name is beyond every doubt as far as I am concerned. If Paul is right (in the quotation from Isaiah [59:20] that he transforms into a reference to the parousia of Christ in Romans 11:26), and the coming redeemer turns out to be Jesus, then all of Israel will surely welcome him as the anointed of the Lord. "Until he comes" (1 Cor. 11:26), we both live in hope that must remain open as long as God does not give us certainty. Just as hard to dispute would be the possibility that God could surprise us both as he has already done so often, "for my thoughts are not your thoughts, neither are your ways my ways, says the Lord" (Is. 55:8).

RAHNER:

Everyone lives in a dialectical relationship with his fellow human beings. He recognizes the other to be as he

is and still has expectations, hopes, and demands that
the other has not yet fulfilled. So you must indulge me
(if I may formulate it so sharply) if I were still to expect
that you would be baptized in this present age.

LAPIDE:

I accept your hope in the same spirit of love and concern for the salvation of my soul in which it is meant
—although I cannot share in it. Likewise I nurse the
hope that when "the Son himself will also be subjected to the [Father] . . . , so that God may be all in
all" (1 Cor. 15:28), on that day "all of them may call
on the name of the Lord and serve him with one accord," as it says in *Nostra Aetate* in the words of
Zephaniah (3:9), and that you also, dear Father
Rahner, and your fellow Christians will become such
monotheists as understood by Judaism.

RAHNER:

Naturally, as long as you are a Jew in your convictions,
you must hope that Christian monotheism will distance
itself from an incarnational alliance with Jesus and in
this way, as you formulated it, God will be all in all.
You must hope for that out of your conviction, as you
must grant me the opposite conviction.

LAPIDE:

I would nevertheless want to go beyond mutual tolera-
tion. For me, Jesus is no insignificant person, one of
many rabbis in Galilee. For thirty years I have occupied
myself with him, his teachings, and the history of his
impact. But many riddles remain unanswered, some of

his features I see only in blurred outline, and his precise identity eludes all research. It is certain for me that he is a bright light of Israel and belongs to the great teachers of humankind. When in church you glorify God with "Halleluja" and conclude your prayers with the Hebrew word "Amen," when Hebraic vocabulary and Hebraic modes of thought run through your theology and your liturgy like a red thread, that is not the least of his merits. The Catholic New Testament scholar Franz Mussner writes: "Jesus makes humanity 'Jewish' insofar as humanity was Christian and becomes Christian, for through him the Jewish categories of thought and faith came into the consciousness of people and works like a fermenting sourdough." If the conversion of humanity to Israel's God is the penultimate goal of world history, the Christianization of a billion people—which happened in Jesus' name—is a significant step forward in the direction of this salvation. It is true that I can not acknowledge Jesus as the Messiah of Israel nor as the redeemer of a still unredeemed world. However, that God availed himself of him in order to bring about a step forward, a progression on the way to redemption, is a fact of more profound theological consequence. I can also not accept his birth as God's incarnation (in the Christian sense of the word), but his exemplary human existence as *vere homo*, which has much to say to us both, can help us to a deepened, more noble human existence. This is and remains the basis for continuing dialogue.

RAHNER:
What you say is an approximation of the Christian teaching about Jesus, an approximation that I can greet

only thankfully. For myself, I would still perhaps suppose that behind your relativism in the interpretation of Jesus there is something else lurking that, if I may formulate it explicitly, you would still reject. However finally and ultimately I must still say once more, first: because Jesus himself promised me God's absoluteness in an irreversible way (which means, that God in his works can neither retreat from this promise nor trump it), everything is already included for me in this future irreversibly promised by Jesus, both in terms of the further possibilities of religion and of my own existence as well, even though I don't know in detail what is already implied. And second I would say: if I believe in Jesus in this way as the irreversible and victorious self-promise of God, I have already actually reached that which the Church's theology of Incarnation teaches. For even in this theology of Incarnation that which is of absolute importance for the Jewish monotheist, and possibly also for the Muslim, is not denied—namely, that God and the creature are two different realities and they remain unmixed even in Jesus with total unity between divinity and humanity.

LAPIDE:

I am grateful to you for this clarification. For fifteen hundred years the average Jew has been of the opinion that "becoming human" and "incarnation" signify for the Christian that the creator of the universe shrank himself completely into the human body of Jesus, in a manner of speaking, in order to become totally flesh and blood. Such a notion for the Jew, however, borders on idolatry or the deification of the creature. It is high time to demolish such faulty interpretations and misunderstandings, which are frequently more semantic than theological in nature, through a candid exchange of ideas. It could be that we will then discover that the chasm which separates Jews and Christians from one another is not half as deep as our forefathers had assumed.

RAHNER:

To that I would say the following, which you may regard as a compliment to the Jews if you like. For me the Incarnation, properly understood (which doesn't signify an identity between divinity and creatureliness, but rather a nevermore dissolvable union between the promising God and creaturely promise), is in a certain sense, and naturally only so, an almost self-evident matter. Especially when for me the end of the creature is only fulfilled by God when the creature, without disappearing, reaches God again—precisely in Jesus and in the deifying grace that comes to people. However, the Incarnation, so understood, occurs precisely in Jesus the Jew (and not in a Buddhist or in some otherwise mystical way), and thus the irrevocable promise of God in history, as opposed to some mystical experience, is given precisely in Jesus the Jew as nowhere else. That is the matchless and exciting conviction of Christianity. I would almost say that the scandal in the Christian message is not a Christology, but rather a Jesus-oriented Christology. To an Indian, for instance, it is self-evident that there is a divine humanity in human being as a whole. And that is not simply false. For if as a Christian I say that the eternal God communicates himself through the uncreated grace that we name the Holy Spirit to every person who will not be damned eternally, then a universal divine humanity is also somehow envisioned. But for me as a Christian the fact still remains that there is a historical self-promise of God in the event of a concrete person and that this happened precisely in Jesus and (please pardon the banality) not in Prussia or India. And this is the concrete experience of Christianity, which cannot be deduced speculatively. This self-promise happened in Judaism.

LAPIDE:

That may belong to the mission of Israel. For if we, "the fewest of all peoples" (Deut. 7:7), were called to transmit to the world the monotheistic faith, the Bible, and the ethos of the prophets as the God-given service to the people of the world, then perhaps Jesus also belongs to those "gifts" that we were destined to bear and pass on. Could you imagine that this mission of Israel's extends even into the future, that further redemptive tasks await us?

RAHNER:

I am no prophet. So strictly speaking I must allow your question to go unanswered. But naturally I hope that Israel helps the balance of humanity to believe further in a prophetic monotheism of God the Father and also Jesus.

BEING CHRISTIAN—
BEING JEWISH

LAPIDE:

One other question that won't leave me in peace concerns the delay of the parousia. The second Letter of Peter indicates that the Christian community could "in lives of holiness and godliness" hasten the arrival of the day of the Lord (2 Pet. 3:11–12). In the Talmud there is an analogous statement: "If all of Israel would keep two Sabbaths in the proper manner, redemption would come immediately." If this is the case, is it not then because of both Christian and Jewish guilt that the redemption so passionately hoped for has still not occurred?

RAHNER:

On theological and perhaps also on Jewish grounds, you could just as easily turn the statement around and say: if God would take the final step toward us Christians and Jews, then as Jews and Christians we would be converted in a way that could permit the final redemption to occur. For a dialectical relationship still obtains between God's action and human freedom, between the efficacious grace of God himself that we cannot manage ourselves and our freedom. However, beyond this point I have yet a further difficulty. Naturally I cannot know what sort of world history (which for me is and always remains a finite one) God actually desires. Thus I can naturally not assert with any certainty that the history of humanity will last another ten thousand years or so longer. However, on the other side, after two thousand years since Jesus, I cannot quite believe that the world history desired by God (and extended not simply through human stupidity and evil) should be so soon at an end. Some things may yet come to pass; people may still discover some things and arrive at historical realizations of human possibilities that we have not yet anticipated. To be sure, everything that can still take place in ongoing history may in a certain sense appear trifling over against the most intrinsic meaning of world history—God himself—even if one has to say again that through these triflings, and only so, can a person attain this final meaning of God himself. And so I believe God still intends to allow many such triflings to occur. Therefore I cannot come to terms with the idea, as the only possibility, that world history and salvation history would already be over if we Jews and Christians behaved in a more Jewish and Christian fashion.

LAPIDE:

That makes sense to me, although I am convinced that it is our duty as religious people to become more human, to sublimate the baser instincts in ourselves, in order to be worthy of the dignity of the image of God. This odious duty to "become human" that is imposed upon us all in order to advance from two-footed mammals to authentic children of God is seminally embedded in our theological vocabulary. In Christianity there is a fine distinction between those who are baptized with water and those who are baptized with the Holy Spirit. In the same way, the prophets distinguish between those who are simply circumsised in the flesh and those whose heart (Jer. 4:4), ears (Jer. 6:10), and lips (Ex. 6:12) are circumsised. Is it not conceivable that being Christian amounts to an ideal that only a very few, like Francis of Assisi and Mother Theresa, have attained, while the majority of nominal Christians are merely en route to total Christianity? In precisely the same way, being Jewish may only reach maturity in the models, like Abraham, Moses, and Rabbi Akiba, while the rest of us Jews lag behind in the hope of achieving authentic Jewish existence through the sweat of our souls. In short, most of us are perhaps still in elementary school when it concerns becoming Jews and becoming Christians.

RAHNER:
Recently I said to young theologians during a retreat that obviously we are baptized in order to become Christians, but we are not simply that already. Thus, as a poet said, we always acknowledge mournfully from afar the one we should be, but aren't. We could become better, though, even if one doesn't interpret the course of history simply as continuous progress and advancement. Whether, for example, as refinement, whether as a better understanding of that which one actually said already, whether as the ever clearer historical and societal objectification of an already intrinsic attitude—that

is not the question here. But it is only naturally the case that every advancement of humanity also produces the possibility of new dreadful possibilities. As long as there was no nuclear fission, there could be no atomic bomb and no Hiroshima. Without current social and technical systems, even the most wicked enemies of the Jews in the Middle Ages could not have produced the horrors that Hitler was able to perform. Democracy is most certainly a positive advance, from which humanity should not retreat. On the other hand, democracy repeatedly produces a "mass" that is roughly the opposite of what it actually championed in the first place. History is and remains a very ambivalent affair.

LAPIDE:

Also fire and water, science and technology, indeed all human undertakings are basically ambivalent and embryonically conceal in themselves blessing as well as curse. I think often of Nicholas of Cusa, who maintained that the world rests on oppositions and contradictions that originated with God and are only reconciled into unity in the return to and absorption in him, their origin and ground. Perhaps these *coincidentia oppositorum* in their earthly stage needed an occasional regression in order effectively to accentuate their original progress.

RAHNER:

The justification of regression (in order to achieve progress later) has certainly been right at times. For me something like that offers small comfort. A Marxist perhaps would say to me that in fifty years we will have a classless society and an earthly paradise will be realized. But I am so important to myself that this idea doesn't console me since I will not be living then. There is still a responsibility that modern liberals and Marxists do not see, a responsibility to and solidarity with the dead, with the underprivileged, whom I cannot regard as simply (pardon the bluntness of the word) the dung of world history out of which grow the flowers and fruit for those who come later.

LAPIDE:

My teacher in Jerusalem used to say: Who is a Jew? A person whom it hurts if one mistreats a black in South Africa, whose stomach growls when a child is hungry in Biafra. Whoever is not capable of suffering with all people may not regard himself as a true Jew.

RAHNER:

And I must also be convinced that those who perished in history still live.

"LIFE AND DEATH, BLESSING AND CURSE . . ."

LAPIDE:

When I contemplate nuclear armaments at present and the endless race to overarm, it appears to me as if behind the whole insanity of opposing plans for mutual annihilation there is a stern rap on the knuckles from above which gives us to understand that humanity has arrived at the crossroad.

"I have set before you life and death, blessing and curse; therefore choose life" (Deut. 30:19), so it says in the Testament of Moses. In today's context, that means: You can create energy and healing from this original force—or war and mass murder. Henceforth the path leads to self-improvement or to self-destruction, and no one takes the burden of choice from you, for the God of freedom has liberated you.

RAHNER:

I believe that a Christian who looks at Jesus and takes seriously his Sermon on the Mount and the foolishness of the cross, in practice and not only in theory, may intercede so that the situation in which we live today can be improved—not through further rearmament, but rather only through disarmament. And that Christians should even have the courage to undertake the spade work.

LAPIDE:

May your words be in the ears of Moscow and Washington!

RAHNER:

Otherwise the madness of the masses, which stands behind all this, continues. And then instantly the fuse is ignited and we have a universal nuclear holocaust.

LAPIDE:

Perhaps the main reason for our misery lies in the fact that humanity has grown warped. In the last millennium it has developed biologically; it has become almost a colossus intellectually, but morally it has remained a dwarf. This disproportion can call forth catastrophic consequences if self-knowledge does not immediately lead us to the imperatives of the moral demand. It appears to me that the grace period of heaven is about to expire.

RAHNER:

Humanity is always discovering better weapons, but must become better morally if a universal misfortune is to be avoided. For me, however, how all these appeals for a higher moral development should actually be formulated and inculcated for there to be hope of their realistic success is a disturbing question that is not genuinely answerable. Many of the appeals of the Church, the popes, and of liberal humanitarians seem so dreadfully cheap to me. When the ecclesiastical appeals of this type strike me as cheap and commonplace, I often console myself as a Catholic with the observation that the nonecclesiastical appeals appear to be as cheap and unrealistic. However, the desperate question remains of why all these moral appeals to a higher ethical development of humanity remain so flimsy and ineffective, although their fulfillment seems to be essential for the fate of humanity. Strictly speaking, I know of no satisfactory answer. I can only hope that if one makes such appeals, admonitions, and entreaties continually afresh, makes them patiently in every possible way, then enough will reach the human race so that the worst will be avoided.

LAPIDE:
The most frequent verb in the vocabulary of Jesus is *to do*. Perhaps we should also transform our burning concern into small actions that promote peace. I recall that great silent protest march in the United States in which priests, rabbis, and pastors marched with Martin Luther King through the state of Mississippi in order to demonstrate opposition to and protest against the discrimination of the colored people. Speechless, unarmed, and defenseless it proceeded, in a common ecumenicity of peace for human rights, which it understood to be about changing powerless solidarity into political power.

RAHNER:

Naturally one cannot always participate in silent marches, underwrite protest statements, and so forth. It is unfortunately the case that even appeals that appear to be remarkable and impressive at the moment quickly bog down and peter out. So one can only continually say, Christians should again and again join forces anew, should continue fighting as well as they are able, should not lose patience, should not give up. Perhaps it will yet help.

THE JEWISH "NO" TO JESUS AS THE CHRIST

LAPIDE:

The importance of this patience brings me back to Jesus. Christians maintain he is the savior of the world. Jews say he is not for us—or at least not yet—the Messiah of Israel. Jesus therefore became a sign of contradiction—between his physical brothers and his spiritual disciples. A contradiction that none of us can resolve before the final redeemer comes. Even Paul admitted that "not all have faith" (2 Thess. 3:2) and warned all rash theologians, "Therefore do not pronounce judgment before . . . the Lord comes!" (1 Cor. 4:5). These are two statements that appeal to me. Still, I believe we should not stop arguing in a brotherly way about Jesus, for new insights and syntheses that strive toward the future emerge only in constructive, dialogical debate. This legitimate brotherly dispute, though, should be conducted under the auspices of the motto of Jesus: "Not everyone who says to me, 'Lord, Lord,' shall enter the kingdom of heaven, but he who does the will of my Father who is in heaven" (Mt. 7:21).

To do the will of our Father in heaven requires no

controversy, for ultimately that is the common concern
of religious Jews and Christians.

RAHNER:
Yes, we should argue further. Despite all the desired
unity that lies in the background, we are simply not
identical in our convictions. However it is part of human decency, of truth and love, that each one confess
the difference in the convictions and still not allow the
dialogue to break off.

LAPIDE:
Entirely right. Here I would like to appropriate a word
of yours that applies to all dialogue partners. With justification you asserted: in the soil of mental laziness, no
piety can flourish. Put differently: whoever believes,
thinks further. Now it is a historical fact that since the
time of early Catholicism the Church has reacted to the
no of the Jews to Jesus as the Christ with a threefold no.
She incorporated a no to the Jews on the part of Christ
into her earliest Scripture and reinforced this through a
no on the part of God to his covenant people—in order
to add a subsequent no on the part of Christendom to
Judaism. Thus evolved a denunciation, rejection, and
disinheritance of Israel by Christian hands, with Jesus
as the ostensible chief witness for an attitude that gives
the lie to his all-encompassing message of love (to say
nothing at all of the love of enemies). Isn't it time to dig
to a deeper level in order to ask ourselves the question:
Could this Jewish no that ultimately originates in faith
and not unbelief have played a positive, God-given role
in the universal plan of salvation?

RAHNER:

Naturally I can confer a positive, constructive significance upon the Jewish no to Jesus in God's plan of salvation. For even if I disregard all the profound theological thoughts about sin and the positive function it has in God's plan of salvation, as a Christian I can say that I have the obligation to interpret this Jewish no to Jesus as the Christ as arising out of a positive relationship to God, although I say no to this no.

LAPIDE:

I thank you for this empathetic solidarity. A whole host of polemical rubbish is herewith cleared away.

RAHNER:

It is now an entirely normal doctrine of Catholic theology that an act that cannot be accepted in terms of its objective content can nevertheless be grounded in an act of faith, even when the content of the act of faith does not yield the objective content of an act grounded in faith. More simply stated: even an act that is not correct in and of itself can come from a subjective command of conscience pleasing to God. Subjective and objective morals are not always identical. If that is the case, then it is naturally self-evident to me that I can recognize a positive redemptive function in this Jewish no that I interpret as a Christian—quite apart from a more profoundly thought out theology of Adam's "fortunate fall." To be sure, I cannot reflect now extemporaneously about precisely wherein the positive redemptive function of the Jewish no consists. It is certainly obvious, though, to a Catholic, for example, that even Luther's no to the Roman Catholic Church has had a positive impact upon the Church. Formulated in a Christian way, where someone stops short with the Old Testament (which is also part of the Christian history of salvation), this can certainly have a positive redemptive function, even if I cannot know precisely in detail wherein this consists. It can indeed be true (perhaps in Goethe's sense) that one has more with less than if one has everything, if everything is expected of one. That grants me no exemption from needing and wanting to have everything. But in any case, I can attribute a positive redemptive function to the decisions dictated by the subjective conscience to stay within the Old Testament.

LAPIDE:

If I may, I would like to carry this breakthrough in the dialogue a step further—naturally on the historical-earthly level, which also belongs to the Almighty's sphere of action. Seen from a human perspective, in order to call the global Church into existence, three indispensable realities were required: the people of Israel in their biblical land, in whose midst the Jew Jesus came into the world, could grow up and mature to manhood, as the Gospels portray it. Likewise required was a small Jewish yes to this Jesus, his teaching and his message in the form of the band of apostles, the primitive community, and the resulting Jesus movement that was composed of several thousand zealous Jews. A second reading of Paul and the Acts of the Apostles, however, also shows that the third precondition was a massive Jewish no in the form of continuing nonacceptance, which the post-Easter Christian preaching of Paul experienced. If we may give credence to the second book of Luke (Acts of the Apostles), this Saul of Tarsus was an inveterate Jewish converter who on his mission trips never neglected in any city to visit first the local synagogue. It happened thus in Iconium (Acts 14:1), in Thessalonica (Acts 17:1), in Beroea (Acts 17:10), in Corinth (Acts 18:4), and in Ephesus (Acts 18:19).

Only after he was rejected with skepticism and condemnation by his "brethren, my kinsmen by race" (Rom. 9:3), in these and other cities did the turning point occur that made Paul the apostle to the Gentiles from Saul the zealous Pharisee. "It was necessary that the word of God should be spoken first to you. Since you thrust it from you," so he said in the synagogue at Antioch, "we turn to the Gentiles" (Acts 13:46).

It is therefore entirely conceivable that if Paul had had any of the success in the synagogues of the Diaspora that he craved so much, he would have had neither enough time nor the desire to turn to the Gentiles. For he never tired of stressing that his first love was for his brothers, the Israelites. Therefore if the Jewish no had not forced Paul into the mission to the Gentiles, it is imaginable—*sit venia verbo!*—that you and the Jesuits in Innsbruck today would still be sacrificing horse meat to the mountain gods of Tirol instead of praying the Hebrew psalms and paying homage to the God of Israel.

RAHNER:
I would like to say the following to that. There are many things in world history and salvation history that

redound from God for the salvation of humankind, although they should not have occurred in the first place and although I am not permitted to do these things simply because they have a redemptive function. Paul enjoins this upon us at the beginning of chapter 6 of the Letter to the Romans. Of course I must immediately add that the positive redemptive function of what should not have occurred is ultimately grounded in Jesus Christ.

LAPIDE:

At the beginning of Romans 6, Paul speaks about continuing "in sin that grace may abound" (Rom. 6:1). In that I reject this view, with him, I am of your opinion. However, behind the Jewish no to Christ is concealed a threefold, resounding yes: A yes to our still unredeemed world in which God has placed us as co-workers in the enterprise of sanctification; a loud yes to the hope for the coming redemption; and a strong yes and amen to the God of the Bible who, come what will, stands by his promises.

In this sense, your colleague Franz Mussner in his book *Tractate on the Jews* frames the basic question— Does Israel still have a redemptive function after Christ?—only in order to answer it affirmatively in seven different ways. In his words: "The Jew is the continuing witness to God in the world and as such . . . for Karl Barth the Jew was the only extrabiblical proof of God to which he [Barth] granted validity. The Jew is the continuing witness to the concreteness of salvation history . . . to the hidden God, whose ways are not discernible. . . . The Jew does not allow the messianic idea to disappear from the world. . . . The Jew holds up the vision of a better world. . . . Israel is the world-historical witness for the not-yet of the divine will and resists the Christian pathos of eschatological time, truth, and judgment. . . . [And not the least:] The history of humanity has become a holy history through Judaism." Out of which he sees the upshot: "The Christian needs the Jew . . . , the Jew helps the Christian to retain his identity, for Israel remains the root of the Church."

Could you agree with that?

RAHNER:
I believe I could agree with that. However I would still say that it concerns the redemptive significance of a fact that I may not elevate into a norm. And if one allows this salvation-historical fact to stand and does not turn it, so to speak, into an absolute of a normative sort, then one must still add that actual Judaism certainly should better fulfill this salvation-historical significance, which you claim for it and I must not dispute, than happens today. In my opinion, God still wants things from the Jews that are unfulfilled.

LAPIDE:
I am completely aware of this. My mistakes, imperfection, and defects as a Jew are often so painfully present to me that many times I am on the point of despairing of my weaknesses. With Paul, I must frequently confess: "I do not do the good I want, but the evil I do not want is what I do" (Rom. 7:19). What helps me get over this all-too-legitimate self-criticism is the rabbinical in-

sight that God's will to forgive is always greater than my ability to sin. Thank God!

However, with the Sermon on the Mount and the Torah ideal, goals are put before us that only a very few are capable of fulfilling completely. The rest of us, the average Jews and the average Christians, do basically what we can, in the hope that our unfulfilled effort may find grace with God.

RAHNER:

May I address another question to you? How far can I regard what you say of Judaism as an actually valid interpretation of Judaism for Jews themselves? If I am asked how Catholic Christianity is to be interpreted authentically, I can refer beyond the New Testament to the councils and other doctrinal clarifications of the Catholic Church. With the question of the properly interpreted essence of Protestant Christianity, I have even more difficulty. And now with you I have a not inconsiderable difficulty. You explain that a very positive relationship to Jesus is still a part of genuine Judaism. Must I think: Mr. Lapide, on his own account and at his own risk, supposes this to be the true essence of Judaism; however, the majority of Jews don't suppose this?

THE JEWISH
INTEREST IN JESUS

LAPIDE:

In my view of Jesus, I can neither speak for all Jews—no one can—nor am I an outsider. The love of Jesus and the academic interest in him and his impact were implanted in me by Jewish teachers like Joseph Klausner, for whom Jesus was "the most Jewish of all Jews," Martin Buber, who perceived him as "his great brother," and Leo Baeck, the last luminary of the German school of rabbis, who in the year 1938 at the time of the Nazi *Kristallnacht* managed to write of him: "We see before us a man who according to all the signs of his personality discloses the Jewish character, in whom the purity and worth of Judaism is so specially and so clearly revealed. . . . Jewish thought, Jewish history may not ignore him . . . not fail to appreciate him, nor here want to disclaim him. Even here Judaism should encompass its own, in order to know its own." In the meantime, many have heeded this admonition. In the last thirty years in the State of Israel alone, 187 Hebrew books on Jesus have appeared—more than in all the previous nineteen centuries combined. If one includes the research on

Jesus of Jewish scholars in Europe and America since 1950, the volume exceeds the three hundred mark. Common to all these Jewish presentations is a growing sense of insight into the life and death of the Nazarene, an empathy that is often scarcely distinguishable from sympathy, and a consciousness of spiritual affinity that calls for a belated "homecoming." The religious zeal of Jesus, his love for all of Israel, and his tragic death— these basic facts have brought him very near to many Jewish thinkers of our generation.

Jews who think, teach, or write about Jesus as I do are certainly still a minority. The trauma of the "Final Solution" still lies all too near; it prompted many to view the cross and the swastika as closely related. From Hitler through Himmler, Eichmann, and the SS troops —virtually all of those actively participating in the genocide were baptized Christians! Nevertheless, the time of generalizations is fading away—one hopes also on the Christian side in terms of their caricatures of Jews and Judaism. The time of a new freedom from bias is beginning. The children of the survivors (and most Jews of my generation understand themselves as survivors) distinguish better between the rabbi of Nazareth who belongs to their flesh and blood, the pseudo-Christians who perverted his good news into a message of menace for his people, and the genuine Christians who are our brothers under God. If more Christians would take the Jewishness of Jesus more seriously, the number of Jews who would be willing to think about his salvific role in the Church would also grow. Yet still one question. "Whoever encounters Jesus Christ encounters Judaism." This statement, as has already been mentioned, begins the most recent declaration of the German bishops on the relationship of the Church to Judaism (of 28 April 1980). What do you think about this laconic, but altogether unambiguous statement?

RAHNER:

In the first place permit me a preliminary observation of a logical sort that sounds somewhat mildly critical. You could take the word *encounter* in both parts of their statement (whose acceptance you wish for) in precisely the same sense. Then the encounter with Jesus, which is essential for me, is to be understood in the sense of Catholic fundamental theology. Then the encounter with the historical Jesus is what is meant. This encounter is for me only the beginning of an experience of encountering Jesus that only comes to its conclusion when the Christ of faith is discovered. When and insofar as I, as a Catholic Christian and a fundamental theologian, must begin the formation of my faith and my fundamental theology concretely with the historical Jesus, as this Jesus is given initially on the first level of historical experience, I naturally encounter a Jewish Jesus in his natural Jewish environment. And in order to find this Jesus, I must want to encounter the Judaism of his time. That is self-evident. When this encounter with Jesus continues into the belief in him as the Messiah, naturally a further interpretation of Judaism (which I encounter in a thoroughly positive way) arises for me that is distinctive from your relationship to Judaism and your interpretation of Judaism.

LAPIDE:

Does the opening statement of the bishops' declaration not signify, then, that the Jewish Jesus is the foundation on which all Christology is based and that his Jewishness is an essential element of his humanity? Certainly there are no ethereal people who walk on the clouds. To every *vere homo* belongs a piece of the earth as home, a mother tongue, a racial identity, and a specific tradition and faith-world. In terms of all these constitutive elements of his humanity, Jesus was a complete, believing Jew who, according to all the Christian sources, wanted to be nothing other than a devout son of Israel. No divine sonship, transfiguration, rapture, and exaltation can detract one iota from his native-born Judaism, render him non-Jewish, or subsequently Christianize him.

RAHNER:

I attribute various significance to the details of my own plural reality—if one compares one to another, although all are given and none can be denied. So also there are in Jesus and in Judaism the most diverse religious and existential realities. If then, for example, Jesus had a beard, then I can always still say that, relatively, that is of no consequence to me. So he could possibly have had Jewish characteristics that in the final analysis are matters of indifference as far as I'm concerned. I concede, though, that for an actual, credible, and radical relationship to Jesus, even his special characteristics, which cannot be derived from an abstract human essence, can be significant. The boundary between such special characteristics in Jesus and others, which remain unimportant for me, appears to me to be not at all precisely specified and can certainly also differ for individual Christians. For example, it could be that there are among us Catholics people who say that, although Jesus was literally poor, this circumstance doesn't concern them especially—Jesus could have been a wealthy landowner in Israel. Other Christians—for example, Francis of Assisi, or Ignatius Loyola, or the theologians of liberation—will say: no, that Jesus was poor and preferred solidarity with the poor and oppressed is a different matter than the style of his beard and has a genuine existential redemptive significance for us to which we must first do justice.

JEWS AND CHRISTIANS—
FRATERNAL OPPONENTS

LAPIDE:
Could it not be that God allowed Jesus to come to the
world as a Jew before he became the Christ of Christendom, that he placed us both—Jews and Christians—in a
dialectical relationship of tension that amounts to a
challenge to reflect together on the often strange and
complex divine paths of salvation? Perhaps two frater-
nal opponents were necessary to scramble nearer the
truth!

RAHNER:
I can grant all that—if it is not overlooked that as a
Christian I recognize Jesus as the unsurpassable Messiah for all. On this question we still differ, and under
this proviso (which must remain explicit), and only so, I
can acknowledge a positive redemptive meaning and effect in the dialectical relationship between Jews and
Christians. And so in an actual way this positive dialectical relationship is nevertheless something that for me
should be superseded by a recognition of Jesus as the
savior of the whole world, and thus also of the Jews.

LAPIDE:

I can understand that, though I would add to what you said a word by Jürgen Moltmann. In his book *The Church in the Power of the Spirit,* he writes: "Through his crucifixion, Jesus became savior of the Gentiles. In his Parousia, however, he will prove himself also to be Israel's Messiah." That seems to me to be a strong formula for reconciliation—until God gives us the fullness of certainty. For if on the day of the Lord it should be revealed that the Christian hope was legitimated, then that should be fair for all religious people. God knows what he is doing and Jews loyal to the Bible trust his will blindly and without question. In the meantime, though, "until he comes" (1 Cor. 11:26), we all live in hope, we travel as pilgrims toward the same Messiah and we build hopefully on one and the same gracious love of God, without which our earthly existence would be meaningless. That is and remains the threefold biblical ecumenicity that binds us Jews and Christians to one another irrevocably—all unconcealed, explicit differences notwithstanding.

RAHNER:

I can accept all that under the presupposition that this perspective on an identity that only occurs eschatologically, and is a legitimate type of comfort to us in our present nonidentity, not exempt us from even now doing everything to bring us still closer together.

LAPIDE:

A half century ago in Stuttgart Martin Buber dreamt: "If Judaism again became Israel . . . , the separation would probably remain undiminished . . . , but not a sharper confrontation between us and the church. Rather something altogether different that is today still inexpressible."

Perhaps he meant this responding one to the other, an opening of oneself to the other, the striving toward one another, taking the other and his religious experience seriously, the harmony in all polyphony and the joy in the duality that knows final unity only in God.

RAHNER:
Mutually we have something to say. Presumably we have not yet satisfactorily said that which we mutually have to say in order that we totally understand each other completely.

LAPIDE:
May this prospective quest for mutual elucidation stand under the auspices of the words of the prophet Malachi, with which I would like to close: "Then those who feared the Lord spoke with one another; the Lord heeded and heard them, and a book of remembrance was written before him of those who feared the Lord and thought on his name. 'They shall be mine, says the Lord of hosts, my special possession, . . . and I will spare them' " (Mal. 3:16–17).